# THE SEVEN EARLY WARNING SIGNS: UNDERSTANDING POST-TRAUMATIC STRESS DISORDER (PTSD)

MASTER THE THERAPEUTIC STEPS FOR RESILIENCE, RECOVERY, AND EMOTIONAL STABILITY

GABRIELLE

**Copyright** © 2024 Gabrielle. All rights reserved.

The content within this book may not be reproduced, duplicated, or transmitted without direct written permission from the author or the publisher.

Under no circumstances will any blame or legal responsibility be held against the publisher or author for any damages, reparation, or monetary loss due to the information contained within this book, either directly or indirectly.

Legal Notice:

This book is copyright protected. It is only for personal use. You cannot amend, distribute, sell, use, quote, or paraphrase any part of the content within this book without the consent of the author or publisher.

Disclaimer Notice:

Please note that the information contained within this document is for educational and informational purposes only. All efforts have been expended to present accurate, up- to-date, reliable, and complete information. No warranties of any kind are declared or implied. Readers acknowledge that the author is not engaged in the rendering of legal, financial, medical, or professional advice. The content within this book has been derived from various sources. Please consult a licensed professional before attempting any techniques outlined in this book.

By reading this document, the reader agrees that under no circumstances is the author responsible for any losses, direct or indirect, that are incurred as a result of the use of the information contained within this document, including, but not limited to, errors, omissions, or inaccuracies.

# TABLE OF CONTENTS

INTRODUCTION ............................................................................... vi
PART ONE UNDERSTANDING PTSD ................................................ 1
CHAPTER 1 WHAT IS PTSD? ............................................................. 2
    TYPES OF PTSD ........................................................................... 3
    GENERAL CONSIDERATIONS ..................................................... 4
CHAPTER 2 C-PTSD STORIES OF HEALING ................................... 6
    LISA'S STORY ............................................................................... 7
    PHILIP'S STORY .......................................................................... 10
CHAPTER 3 BABY BOOMERS AND PTSD ...................................... 12
    CAUSAL FACTORS IN CIVILIAN PTSD .................................... 13
    CAUSAL FACTORS IN MILITARY PTSD ................................. 15
PART TWO THE SEVEN EARLY WARNING SIGNS OF PTSD ..... 19
CHAPTER 4 EMOTIONAL DYSREGULATION ............................... 20
    EMOTIONAL DYSREGULATION .............................................. 20
    Dialectical Behavioral Therapy ...................................................... 21
    NEGATIVITY SYNDROME ......................................................... 21
CHAPTER 5 INTRUSIVE THOUGHTS ............................................. 23
    Flashbacks ...................................................................................... 23
CHAPTER 6 AVOIDANCE AND DETACHMENT ............................ 26
    AVOIDANCE ................................................................................ 26
    DETACHMENT OR NUMBING .................................................. 28
        SAMUEL'S STORY ................................................................. 29
CHAPTER 7 PHYSICAL SYMPTOMS OF PTSD .............................. 31
    SKIN PROBLEMS ........................................................................ 31
    SLEEP PROBLEMS ..................................................................... 32
    RINGING IN THE EARS .............................................................. 32
    HEARING DIFFICULTIES .......................................................... 32

- WEIGHT GAIN .................................................................. 32
- DIGESTIVE PROBLEMS ................................................... 33
- ACHES AND PAINS ......................................................... 33
- MUSCLE DEVELOPMENT ................................................ 33
- COLD EXTREMITIES ....................................................... 34
- EXCESSIVE YAWNING ................................................... 34
- ALLERGIES ..................................................................... 34
- HEART DISEASE ............................................................. 34

CHAPTER 8 COGNITIVE CHANGES .................................. 35
- ATTENTIONAL DIFFICULTIES ....................................... 35
- IMPAIRED MEMORY ..................................................... 35
- EXECUTIVE DYSFUNCTION ......................................... 36
- COGNITIVE CHANGES .................................................. 36
- EMOTIONAL DYSREGULATION ................................... 36

CHAPTER 9 PTSD AND SELF-DESTRUCTIVE BEHAVIOR .......... 38

CHAPTER 10 INTERPERSONAL RELATIONSHIPS ....................... 41
- FRIENDSHIPS ................................................................. 41
- SPOUSAL ADJUSTMENT ................................................ 42
- EMPLOYMENT ............................................................... 44
  - A SPOUSE'S STORY .................................................... 45

PART THREE THERAPEUTIC STEPS FOR RECOVERY ............... 47

CHAPTER 11 THERAPIES ..................................................... 48
- GROUP THERAPY .......................................................... 48
  - DANIEL'S STORY ........................................................ 50
- MEDICATION-ASSISTED THERAPY ............................... 50
- TRANSCRANIAL MAGNETIC STIMULATION ................. 51

CHAPTER 12 CBT AND EMDR ............................................. 53
- COGNITIVE BEHAVIORAL THERAPY ............................ 53
- EMDR ............................................................................ 56

HISTORY AND TREATMENT PLANNING ............................................. 57
    BRIAN'S STORY .................................................................... 57
    HARRY'S STORY ................................................................... 59
    JILL'S STORY ......................................................................... 60
    JOHN'S STORY ..................................................................... 61
You Have Been Through Darkness and Can Now See the Light—Not Everyone Has ............................................................................................ 63

# CHAPTER 13 SOMATIC EXPERIENCING AND RTM THERAPY . 66
  SOMATIC EXPERIENCING ........................................................ 66
    Workplace Bullying ................................................................. 73
    Developmental Trauma ........................................................... 73
    Releasing Rage ........................................................................ 73
  RECONSOLIDATION OF TRAUMATIC MEMORIES ................. 74
    RAY'S STORY ........................................................................ 75
    KENNETH'S STORY ............................................................. 76
    JORGE'S STORY ................................................................... 76
    ROBERT'S STORY ................................................................ 77

# CHAPTER 14 MINDFULNESS MEDITATION, YOGA, AND HYPERBARIC OXYGEN THERAPY (HBOT) ................................... 79
  MINDFULNESS MEDITATION .................................................... 79
  YOGA ........................................................................................... 82
  HYPERBARIC OXYGEN THERAPY (HBOT) ............................ 82

# CHAPTER 15 ART THERAPY AND WRITING THERAPY .... 84
  ART THERAPY ............................................................................ 84
  WRITING THERAPY ................................................................... 86
    MARIA'S STORY .................................................................. 90
    HANNAH'S STORY .............................................................. 91
    JESSICA'S STORY ................................................................ 93
    ERIC'S STORY ...................................................................... 94

BILL TAYLOR'S STORY ................................................. 95

HUZE'S STORY ............................................................ 96

JOE DEVERA'S STORY ................................................. 97

SHIGEKO'S STORY ....................................................... 99

PART FOUR CULTIVATING RESILIENCE AND EMOTIONAL STABILITY ................................................................. 101

CHAPTER 16 DAILY ROUTINES AND NUTRITIONAL HELP ........................................................................... 102

    DAILY ROUTINES ................................................... 102

CHAPTER 17 SEEKING HELP AND CREATING A SUPPORT NETWORK .................................................................. 107

    CREATING A SUPPORT NETWORK ......................... 107

    TIPS FOR SUPPORTING SOMEONE WITH PTSD ......... 107

    LICENSED PRACTITIONERS FOR PTSD .................. 110

    Imagine a World Where PTSD Wasn't Something We Brushed Under the Rug But Instead…Fought Together! ............. 113

CONCLUSION ............................................................. 115

REFERENCES ............................................................. 117

# INTRODUCTION

Several years ago, I met a new friend named Rose, a fitting appellation because she was like a vibrant flower blooming with intensity. After I visited her at her nearby home, we became fast friends. Soon, because our lives were so busy, we fell out of contact. Now and then, I felt the urge to call but didn't want to be the first one to reach out.

When Rose finally called me, she said words I'll never forget because of the pure anguish in her voice. "Gabrielle, I don't know what's wrong with me." Rose reached out to me because she had the early signs of post-traumatic stress disorder (PTSD). I identified with her because I previously had the same symptoms.

Rose suffered from trauma because she lacked an emotional connection with her dad. My trauma stemmed from years of dealing with our son's depression and drug abuse. Though we believed we'd moved past these circumstances, the scars left on a primal level were too deep for our bodies to forget.

I found PTSD to be parasitic. It latched onto me and destroyed my mind.

Trauma can wreak havoc on your life. Triggered behavioral turbulence can affect your productivity and harm your relationships. You may have emotional scars that will escalate if not addressed. Though professional help is necessary, you may fear opening old wounds.

Do you have the diagnosis?

This book will dispel your fears by highlighting the seven early warning signs of PTSD. Finally, it will serve as a guide to the best therapeutic approaches for ensuring a healthy recovery.

**Part One** discusses the definitions, prevalence, and types of PTSD. The research centers on the baby boomer population, ages 58-76.

**Part Two** breaks down the emotional and psychological changes associated with the seven early warning signs. These signs include intrusive thoughts, detachment (or numbing), avoidance, emotional dysregulation, negativity alteration, and physical and cognitive changes. I also address changes in interpersonal relationships and symptoms of destructive behavior.

**Part Three** explores the following treatments recommended by the American Psychological Association (APA): cognitive behavior therapy (CBT), transcranial magnetic stimulation (TMS), eye movement desensitization and reprocessing (EMDR), group therapy, somatic therapy, art therapy, and writing therapy. Though not yet officially endorsed, I address the reconsolidation of traumatic memories (RTM), meditation, and yoga. The medications conditionally recommended for the treatment of PTSD are sertraline, paroxetine, fluoxetine, and venlafaxine (APA, 2020).

**Part Four** focuses on practical steps for healing and healthy life skills development. I include suggestions on how to find a doctor who will take your symptoms seriously.

I include personal, real-life accounts of PTSD sufferers who found total healing. Interspersed in their stories are personal anecdotes in which I compare our journeys. The healing protocols referenced in each of these stories are found in Part Three.

# PART ONE
# UNDERSTANDING PTSD

# CHAPTER 1
# WHAT IS PTSD?

Post-traumatic stress disorder (PTSD) is a chronic, often debilitating mental health disorder that can develop after a traumatic event, such as military combat, a natural disaster, sexual assault, or the unexpected loss of a loved one. For many people, the symptoms resolve within several weeks. However, approximately 10 to 20 percent of individuals have symptoms that persist and are associated with impairment (Mayo Clinic, 2022; NIMH, 2024).

An estimated one in 11 people will be diagnosed with PTSD in their lifetime (Veterans Affairs, 2023). Though statistics vary, in the general adult population, the lifetime prevalence of PTSD is about eight percent, which highlights the unique difficulties older people experience (SingleCare Team, 2024). Women are twice as likely as men to have PTSD. Of the 70 percent interviewed who experienced at least one traumatic event, one out of three people developed PTSD.

The five symptom clusters from the Diagnostic and Statistical Manual of Mental Disorders (DSM) are emotional dysregulation, detachment or numbing, intrusive thoughts, avoidance, and negativity syndrome. In addition to these five, I will discuss physical and cognitive changes, bringing the total number of warning signs to seven (American Psychiatrist Association, 2024).

For a PTSD diagnosis, you must experience one, two, or more of the symptoms listed in each group cluster for one month or longer (and not as a result of medication, substance use, or illness). The symptoms are usually pronounced enough to cause considerable distress or difficulty in multiple areas of your life.

Certain factors can contribute to your risk, such as the severity and duration of the trauma, the availability of a support network, and the number of traumas you have witnessed (American Psychiatric Association, 2013).

## TYPES OF PTSD

Secondary PTSD (S-PTSD), also known as secondary traumatic stress (STS), occurs when you learn that a relative or close friend has experienced trauma. You can develop the condition from watching someone else, a phenomenon also called vicarious trauma (Bride, Ridley & Figley, 2007; Hensel, Ruiz, Finney & Dewa, 2015).

Delayed expression is a DSM specifier when symptoms appear years after the traumatic event. Many baby boomers present symptoms decades after the initial circumstance. Even if the diagnosis entity did not exist, the symptoms could have existed throughout the adult's lifetime. The symptoms can resemble other mental health conditions, such as depression or anxiety. A meta-analysis found that delayed expression of PTSD is more likely to occur because of child abuse (Friedman, 2013).

Cloitre, Garvert, Weiss, Carlson, and Bryant stated that complex PTSD (C-PTSD) is a category of PTSD with three additional clusters of significant symptoms: emotional dysregulations, negative self-beliefs (e.g., feelings of shame, guilt, failure for wrong reasons), and interpersonal difficulties. Symptoms of C-PTSD are prolonged feelings of terror, worthlessness, helplessness, distortions in identity or sense of self, and hyper-vigilance. These symptoms share similarities with borderline personality disorder, dissociative identity disorder, and somatization (2014).

The concept of C-PTSD was introduced in 1988 by Dr. Judith Herman, a Harvard psychiatrist whose work helped raise awareness of the strong association between childhood adversity and its long-term effects on physical and mental health in adult years. The symptoms are severe within this category (Barry, 2023).

## GENERAL CONSIDERATIONS

PTSD can have a significant influence on your mental health, causing a wide range of symptoms affecting your daily life. Depression, anxiety, panic, fear, and insomnia can cause you to lose interest in activities you previously enjoyed. Intrusive thoughts, such as flashbacks and nightmares, can impair your functioning.

If you suffer from traumatic memories, you may have difficulty maintaining relationships with friends and family. Your symptoms can cause problems with trust, closeness, communication, and problem-solving. Your family may suffer if you cannot complete everyday tasks. Partners and children may feel stressed when communication becomes challenging. Being easily startled, avoiding social situations, and having nightmares can take a toll on even your most caring family members.

Trauma survivors often engage in self-destructive behaviors such as substance abuse, self-harm, excessive gambling, and aggression. This cluster of the DSM-5 highlights the importance of understanding the interplay of self-destructive behavior and PTSD (American Psychiatric Association, 2024).

The economic burden of PTSD is comparable to that of other mental health conditions. Increased awareness of PTSD, the development of more effective therapies, and the expansion of evidence-based interventions may be warranted to reduce the significant clinical and economic burden (Davis et al., 2022).

The American Psychological Association (2020) recommends the following treatment options: cognitive behavior therapy (CBT), group therapy, transcranial magnetic stimulation (TMS), eye movement desensitization and reprocessing (EMDR), meditation, and yoga. Though not officially endorsed, I address the Reconsolidation of

Traumatic Memories (RTM) protocol. The APA-approved medicines for PTSD are sertraline, paroxetine, fluoxetine, and venlafaxine.

People with PTSD who sought early treatment had symptoms lasting an average of 36 months (3 years), while those who did not seek treatment had symptoms lasting an average of 64 months (Grinage, 2023). While approximately one-third of people do not achieve complete symptom elimination with treatment, most individuals experience a significant reduction in the intensity of their symptoms.

One study found that as many as 46 percent of people with PTSD improved within six weeks of beginning psychotherapy (Morina, Koerssen & Pollet, 2016). Researchers have found that as many as 62 percent of people receiving medication for PTSD show improvement.

# CHAPTER 2
# C-PTSD STORIES OF HEALING

I have included the following stories to show that even the most severe cases can have successful outcomes.

Because a C-PTSD diagnosis takes time to manifest, recovery calls for dedication. Years of abuse and trauma may be a part of your past.

The following steps are guidelines for treatment:

Establish security and stability in healing. If you don't feel protected, you won't be able to start your C-PTSD recovery.

Therapy can be a trigger because it requires relating to another person. You will not be punished for expressing your thoughts or feelings. Mental, emotional, and physical support are essential for healing. You may need to return to safety and stabilization during the healing process (Hoffman, Asnaani, Vonk, Sawyer & Fang, 2012).

You should take part in mourning and remembrance. Many trauma survivors never fully recover because of skipping this phase of the process. Healing will result only when memories are resolved and reconsolidated. A competent trauma therapist can help you through this phase with gentle guidance and make sure that remembering doesn't become too much to handle. This process is about redefining and rediscovering who you are (Herman, 2015).

Instead of feeling powerless and perpetually victimized, you can find a new voice. Often, C-PTSD gives rise to a sense of purpose through service to others. Giving back helps any recovery work. Ultimately, this step is all about forward-thinking and no longer dwelling on the past (Quirke, 2024).

**LISA'S STORY**

Nine years after Lisa killed an intruder who had broken into her house, she began noticing PTSD symptoms. Even though her symptoms were delayed, her treatment was successful.

As with Lisa, my PTSD symptoms were delayed. Years after our son's recovery, I experienced the full force of what we, as parents, had endured. At first, because of his privacy concerns, I limited how much I shared with others. Later, after writing about our son in a spiritual memoir, I was comfortable revealing his progress.

Lisa enjoyed her job as a police officer, working the night shift in Spring, Texas. On Monday, August 8, 2011, she ended her morning shift and went for a run in her neighborhood. After showering, Lisa went to bed around 8 a.m. Her alarm was set for 4 p.m. because she was in law school and had to study for summer finals.

She fell asleep wearing a white tank top and black skivvies. At noon, Lisa woke up to a thump at her bedroom window. Something was scratching the screen. Lisa didn't have an alarm because she lived in a quiet neighborhood with very little crime. When she realized that someone was breaking in, she threw on her glasses and ran to the garage, where she grabbed her shotgun, a Remington 870, 12-gauge pump-action firearm. It was fully loaded. She typically kept her firearm handy, but this day, she foolishly left it in the garage.

Lisa ran through the house and stopped at the back door to catch her breath. She opened the door and stepped out onto the patio. She scanned the yard, looked to her left, and saw her bedroom window screen on the ground. Lisa moved toward the alley on the left side of her house. As she slowly cleared the corner, she saw him. He was a white male, approximately 6 feet tall, wearing a striped shirt, jeans, and grey gloves. He was much bigger than Lisa, and she was afraid.

She pointed her shotgun at him, yelling for him to get on the ground. Though the man held up his hands, he was inching closer. He lunged and snatched her shotgun's barrel, whipping her body around as she gripped the stock. Her glasses flew off, and they both tumbled to the purple concrete pavers.

Lisa felt like time and space had melted away, and so began what she called the worst moment of her life. He was on top, crushing her. He kept yanking the shotgun, trying to pull it from her sweaty hands. He dragged her from side to side. The concrete tore her legs, back, and elbows.

He grunted in her ear that he was going to kill her. Lisa was in her fight-or-flight mode and just held on. She looked up at the sky through her pergola's vines. Sometimes, she goes back to imagining that she died at that moment.

"At times, I wanted to die. I grew up very sheltered and had difficulty admitting that I had a problem child. Early on, he had problems at school and in the neighborhood, but much of this was due to his depression."

The attacker was overpowering Lisa, and somehow, her lungs filled with air. He stood up and backpedaled, but he still faced her. Lisa, afraid he was going to come after her again, sprang up and squeezed the trigger. The cannon blasted gunshots. He hunched over and fell.

Lisa ran inside, her fingers shaking, dialed 911, and grabbed her other backup pistol: a Ruger LCP .380 caliber. She thought there would be more intruders. She heard neighbors calling her outside. The officers arrived minutes later.

She was hysterical and kept asking if the perpetrator was in custody. She worried that he had run away, but the officer said he was dead. After they treated her wounds and calmed her down, one of the EMTs knelt and whispered that he was gone.

As is common among trauma survivors, Lisa couldn't remember much at first. The next few days, months, and years were a blur. She remembered how friends, family, and complete strangers contacted her.

Lisa's boyfriend proposed a week later. Lisa spent years trying to distract herself with one milestone after another—marriage, a new career, and a new house. She had three daughters and many projects, but things kept getting more challenging. Lisa went off her selective serotonin reuptake inhibitor (SSRI) because she couldn't focus on her work. I can identify with Lisa's need to focus.

I can identify with Lisa's need to focus on projects. I, too, was on an adrenaline rush. I obsessively volunteered for years, serving on boards and foundations. This helped me in the short run but ultimately proved detrimental.

Lisa changed her work pattern. Lisa returned to patrol but could not ride solo. She partnered with someone who was a much better driver than she was. She left the patrol and worked in homicide for a few years.

Lisa went to therapists within her insurance network but found it hard to make a connection. She was prescribed a generic selective serotonin reuptake inhibitor (SSRI) that treats depression and anxiety. Unfortunately, a few therapy sessions were not enough to keep her from being dragged down into what she called a personal hellhole.

We struggled to find appropriate professional help. For years, our family worked with a psychiatrist whom we loved and respected. In due course, he led us down the wrong path by suggesting a form of tough love that created yet another layer of family dysfunction.

By the fall of 2019, Lisa knew something had to change. She found a new therapist, who prescribed an excellent antidepressant. She was so comfortable in the relationship that she attended therapy every week. Her doctor suggested that Lisa target what was hidden beneath her iceberg—PTSD.

Lisa, like many, admitted that she was ashamed of her story, her secret, and her issues. She feared that if she got a diagnosis of PTSD and said those letters out loud, they would become tattooed on her forehead. Over time, however, she came to realize that if she did not accept the diagnosis, she would never be healed.

Lisa completed four sessions of EMDR in four weeks, that is, one session per week. The first session was hard because she had to retrieve the scary box of memories that she wanted to keep locked up forever. Her discomfort level was at 10 on a 1 to 10 scale. The second session was more accessible. The third was a bit easier. By the fourth session, she could recall those same horrifying memories, but without the horror. She knew it was over, and she was safe. After many years, she finally felt healthy and happy (Priest, 2011).

### PHILIP'S STORY

Philip suffered from PTSD for as long as he could remember. He looks back and laughs because everyone thought he had the perfect life. Unbeknownst to them, he was terrorized by an undiagnosed, debilitating mental illness.

I can relate. I was a beauty queen and won numerous student council awards during my high school years. Despite this, I had few genuine friends and was lonely. Even though I had a stellar reputation on the outside, I wreaked havoc on the home front, terrorizing my family by overreacting to my parents' strict rules. I had difficulty syncing and integrating the two sides of my nature.

Philip had a childhood laced with physical, cognitive, and sexual abuse, as well as an attack at knifepoint that left him thinking that he would die. He would never be the same after the attack. He went to the police to file a report and was interviewed by a counselor but declined their help, thinking he didn't need it. He later admitted that it was the worst decision of his life.

For months, Philip couldn't close his eyes without envisioning the face of his attacker. He suffered horrific flashbacks and nightmares. Even four years after the attack, Philip was unable to sleep alone in his house. He checked windows, doors, and locks obsessively. By the age of 17, he suffered his first panic attack and could not leave his apartment for weeks. Typically social, he stopped trying to make friends or get involved in the community. He often felt confused, forgetting where or who he was. He would panic on the freeway and become unable to drive. He felt as if he had completely lost his mind.

I became completely disoriented when I heard that our son had vanished from his third treatment center. While driving on the highway, I lost my bearings and had to stop. In fact, every time our son relapsed, I felt numb.

I reverted to isolation every time our son's problems worsened. I feared having to answer questions about his condition. No one knew the private hell our family was experiencing. I avoided meeting with friends who would inevitably brag about their children's accomplishments.

Finally, Philip received the diagnosis of C-PTSD. He felt tremendous relief when he realized his condition was treatable. He felt safe for the first time in his thirty-two years. Taking medication and undergoing behavioral therapy marked the turning point in regaining control of his life; He had a satisfying career as an artist and was enjoying his life (Philips, 2009).

*****

# CHAPTER 3
# BABY BOOMERS AND PTSD

Baby boomers are a generational cohort of adults in their late 50s to late 70s. They are all between the Silent Generation and Generation X. This book will target baby boomers, especially those between the ages of 70 and 78.

In the general adult population, the lifetime prevalence of PTSD is about 8 percent, which highlights the unique difficulties that older people experience (American Psychiatric Association, 2024.).

According to community surveys, the current rates of PTSD among baby boomers are between one and a half percent and four percent, which is notable but at a comparatively lower ratio to the adult population as a whole (APA, 2024). Understanding and treating this condition among baby boomers is vital as society struggles with its aging population.

The term "baby boomer" refers to the post-World War II boom in the U.S. population. Lives that were put on hold during the war quickly resumed, with many people choosing to settle down, get married, buy a home, and start a family. In general, this population takes a skeptical approach toward mental health treatment (Kanitz, 2023).

Because many of them place a high priority on being self-sufficient, seeking treatment connotes moral failure. Since many mental health issues were researched while the baby boomers were coming of age, this group faces a significant learning curve in how to talk about these problems healthily. To boomers, the term mental illness refers to only the most severe cases, which would be placed in a mental institution (Santrock, 2020).

A significant proportion of older people struggle with subclinical levels of PTSD without entirely fitting the diagnostic criteria. These symptoms occur in seven to 15 percent of this population, indicating that older adults may have a widespread but underdiagnosed problem (Davis et al., 2020).

## CAUSAL FACTORS IN CIVILIAN PTSD

People don't think of civilian PTSD as being in the same league as military PTSD. Yet up to 80 percent of people will experience at least one trauma, such as an assault, traffic accident, or natural disaster in their lifetime. The more traumatic experiences you have, the more likely you are to have PTSD.

Dealing with death and loss can lead to PTSD. Deep sadness and terror can impair mental health and day-to-day functioning. Because conversations about death are no longer taboo, there has been a shift in the way baby boomers cope. Today, baby boomers may spend a significant amount of time pondering their mortality and the meaning of life (Wick, 2021).

Events such as hurricanes and earthquakes can cause PTSD. The psychological effects might last long after the relief work is completed. In the aftermath of Hurricane Katrina, mental health problems in New Orleans quadrupled. A 2012 study found that participants continued to experience psychological discomfort four years later (McLaughlin et al., 2011).

Medical trauma can cause PTSD. Beeping monitors, constant questioning from the medical staff, and sleep deprivation can be disruptive. The emotional trauma of surviving a near-death experience can be overwhelming even when physical health returns; emotional symptoms can be long-lasting. After being discharged from the hospital, mental fogginess, forgetfulness, and irritability can result (APA, 2024).

Birth trauma can cause PTSD. This is a condition that affects women who have experienced physical or emotional distress during or after childbirth. This may be caused by a lack of support, a long and challenging labor, fear for the baby's life, or an unplanned C-section. Physical complications such as hemorrhaging, the use of forceps, or the use of a vacuum extractor during delivery can be traumatizing. However, recent advances in psychopharmacology have helped women suffering from postpartum depression (APA, 2024).

Societal stressors can cause significant trauma. Judith G. Edersheim, J.D., M.D., is Co-Director and Co-Founder of The Center for Law, Brain & Behavior (Edersheim, n.d). She claims that America, as a nation, suffers from PTSD. Current statistics suggest that the prevalence of PTSD in America makes it the fifth most common psychiatric illness. By contrast, rates are much lower in other Westernized countries like Germany or Spain. Especially at risk are those people who grew up in stressful and uncertain environments, like the inner cities, where rates of trauma are incredibly high.

Events like those at the Pulse in Orlando or any of the 58 mass shootings highlight the conventionally combat-like situations people experience or witness. Research following the September 11, 2001, World Trade Center attack demonstrates that witnessing disasters, even on television, is enough to trigger PTSD. Also, natural disasters like Hurricane Katrina and the recent flooding in West Virginia can directly affect thousands.

There is fear of new terror attacks as well as rampant domestic gun violence. There is trauma over the fact that 2.2 million people are behind bars, a highly disproportionate number of whom are people of color.

People living in inner-city Chicago and similar neighborhoods in Detroit, Washington, D.C., and Atlanta have rates of PTSD equivalent to those seen in soldiers returning from Iraq and Afghanistan. This means that, in terms of mental health outcomes, it is as if these residents live in a war zone. The consequences of high rates of PTSD contribute to community dysfunction and mass incarceration.

Children who are victims of violence experience alienation from their communities and, in the absence of adequate support systems, are at a higher risk of substance abuse, behavioral issues, and, ultimately, arrest and incarceration (Margolin & Gordi, 2000).

## CAUSAL FACTORS IN MILITARY PTSD

Forrest, Edwards, and Daraganova point out that after World War II, returning veterans were often emotionally unavailable. Even though PTSD wasn't a term until the 1980s, many of these fathers had the diagnosis. Reflecting the avoidance cluster, these fathers, having low positive engagement with their children, caused them to feel neglected and unloved. Children who witness their parents' PTSD episodes can develop secondary traumatic stress (STS) due to fear and concern. These issues need to be addressed to prevent developmental problems (2018).

Baby Boomers returning from Vietnam saw firsthand how the war divided American society. Those who served were often treated as traitors instead of heroes. Many in the United States who hadn't planned on attending college suddenly signed up to avoid the draft. This led to a spike in college enrollment, up to 7 percent higher than usual. Some got drafted into the military. The GI Bill, which helps with education costs for vets, offered less than veterans received in earlier wars (Card & Lemieux, 2001).

Vietnam veterans who saw combat are more likely to have marriage problems. They might end up divorcing more often, affecting their long-term health. Being away from family for a long time weakens the bond with their spouses and kids.

Though combat is connected to psychological trauma, the relationship is a complicated one. Sebastian Junger is an American journalist, author, and filmmaker who has reported in the field on dangerous occupations and infantry combat. He covered the War in

Afghanistan for more than a decade. Junger's works explore themes such as brotherhood and trauma as told from the far reaches of human experience. Although Junger is slightly younger than the target audience in this book, his insights hold valid for baby boomers who returned from Vietnam (Junger, 2022).

Junger analyzes trauma not in terms of reliving violent memories but in terms of missing the camaraderie that existed among soldiers in the field. He believes that collaborating for the good of others is beneficial for all. In other words, courage works—the size or the strength of the people or the army is not always central to whether it succeeds (Zorzi, 2023).

Group affiliation and cooperation are adaptive because they trigger a surge in the neuropeptide called oxytocin. This hormone creates a glow of well-being and promotes greater trust and bonding. Hominids rewarded with oxytocin for cooperating must have out-fought, out-hunted, and out-bred the ones that didn't. Those are the hominids from which modern humans are descended (Bourke, 2016).

According to a study conducted by Nagasawa, Mitsui, Ohtani, and Sakuma (2015), the feedback loop of oxytocin and group loyalty creates an expectation that members will self-sacrifice to contribute to group welfare. There may be no better description of a soldier's ethos than that. One of the most noticeable things about life in the military is that you are virtually never alone: day after day, month after month, you are close enough to speak to, if not touch, a dozen or more people. You eat together, sleep together, laugh together, and suffer together. That level of intimacy duplicates our evolutionary past very closely and must create a nearly continual oxytocin reward system (Donadon et al., 2018). He couldn't quite explain what was wrong, but he was far more scared than he'd ever been in Afghanistan (Junger, 2015).

For the next several months, Junger had panic attacks when he was with too many people—airplanes, ski gondolas, crowded bars. In a casual conversation with a psychotherapist, he was asked whether he was affected by his war experiences; he answered "no." But when he mentioned the panic attacks in the subway, she told him about the symptoms of PTSD (Junger, 2015).

I find it interesting that Israel, with mandatory national service and two generations of intermittent warfare, has a PTSD rate as low as one percent. Israel is arguably the only modern country that retains a sufficient sense of community to mitigate the effects of combat on a mass scale. In Israel, veterans benefitted from what could be called the shared public meaning of a war.

Such public meaning—often in more communal, tribal societies—may be due to having a national military service and having the combat zone virtually on their doorstep. Those who returned from combat were re-integrated into a society with a shared experience (Zorzi, 2023).

Many veterans function well during most of their lives but begin to reflect more on their wartime experiences as they age. This reflection process, common in older adults, can trigger PTSD symptoms. The diagnosis is called late-onset stress symptomatology (LOSS), with symptoms including nightmares, flashbacks, avoidance of reminders of the event, heightened startle response, and a loss of interest in activities (Veterans Affairs, 2013).

Several factors can contribute to an increase in PTSD symptoms with age:

- Retirement can exacerbate symptoms due to more free time and fewer distractions from traumatic memories.
- Declining health and strength can also worsen symptoms.
- Current events, such as war news, can trigger painful memories.

Veterans who previously used alcohol or substances to cope with stress may find their symptoms intensify if they quit without adopting healthier coping mechanisms (Veterans Affairs, 2023)

LOSS shares similarities with PTSD but generally involves fewer and less severe symptoms. While some are troubled by these memories, others find that reflecting on their wartime experiences helps them find meaning (Kendall, n.d.).

*****

# PART TWO
# THE SEVEN EARLY WARNING SIGNS OF PTSD

# CHAPTER 4
# EMOTIONAL DYSREGULATION

## EMOTIONAL DYSREGULATION

Emotional dysregulation occurs when you're unable to manage your emotional responses. This means it's difficult to soothe yourself when you feel overwhelmed, sad, or angry, and you find it hard to return to "normal" after these feelings come up (Pedersen, 2022).

People with emotional dysregulation often try to decrease their emotional distress with harmful behaviors, including substance abuse, self-harm, suicidal ideation, and impulsivity (Dibdin, 2022).

According to the experts, the signs and symptoms of emotional dysregulation include the following:

- Being easily overwhelmed and feeling overly emotional
- Crying easily or feeling upset for "no reason" frequent mood shifts
- Impulsivity
- Finding it hard to deal with stress perfectionism
- Angry outbursts
- High levels of anxiety and depression
- High levels of shame and disordered eating
- Self-harm behaviors
- Suicidal thoughts or actions

- Substance misuse
- Relationship conflict

## DIALECTICAL BEHAVIORAL THERAPY

Dialectical behavioral therapy (DBT) — a type of cognitive behavioral therapy (CBT) — is one of the most effective methods for treating emotional dysregulation. Originally developed for treating borderline personality disorder (BPD), this therapy can help individuals learn new strategies for regulating their emotions, managing conflicts, and building their tolerance for unpleasant feelings (Malas & Gómez-Domenech, 2024).

## NEGATIVITY SYNDROME

Negativity syndrome manifests as an absolute belief in self-esteem, trust, danger, and intimacy, lacking a middle ground. The just-world belief, a concept used in cognitive processing therapy, helps you unlearn the idea that good things happen to good people and bad things happen to bad people. Reality is more nuanced.

Over time, people adjust this belief, but those with PTSD may rigidly adhere to it or completely reject it. If they cling to it, they may blame themselves for the trauma, leading to low self-esteem or perfectionism. If they reject the just-world belief, they may view the world as entirely dangerous and feel powerless, becoming reclusive and distrusting (Psylaris, 2021).

While it is important to reassure trauma victims that they are not at fault, clinicians should avoid pushing this point. Some patients may hold on to guilt because it is easier to bear than helplessness. Self-blame implies some control over the trauma, suggesting that different future choices could prevent recurrence.

Sandy (2010) stated that experts say that negativity syndrome may include the following behaviors:

1. Inability to recall important aspects of the traumatic event. This can be due to dissociative amnesia, not due to head injury, drugs, or alcohol.
2. Persistent and distorted negative beliefs or expectations about yourself or the world, such as "I am bad" or "The world is perilous."
3. Persistent distorted cognition that leads you to blame yourself for the traumatic event.
4. Persistent negative emotional state, including fear, guilt, anger, or shame.
5. Markedly diminished interest in significant activities that used to be enjoyable.
6. Feelings alienated, estranged, or detached from others.
7. Persistent inability to experience a positive emotion such as happiness, satisfaction, or love.

# CHAPTER 5
# INTRUSIVE THOUGHTS

Intrusive memory is perhaps the most distinctive and readily identifiable symptom of PTSD. For survivors, the traumatic event remains, sometimes for decades or a lifetime, retaining its power to evoke panic, terror, dread, grief, or despair. Flashbacks or night terrors increase physical excitation and stress, leading to changes in body temperature, heartbeat, and blood pressure (APA, 2013; NIMH, n.d.).

Intrusive symptoms refer to recurrent, distressing remembrances such as nightmares and flashbacks. According to the DSM-5-TR criteria, a PTSD diagnosis must include at least one intrusive-memory symptom. In a 2018 study involving 166 people with PTSD, 49 percent of participants experienced painful flashbacks. In a 2023 study involving 398 people with PTSD or C-PTSD (Gilles, 2018), about 92 percent of participants reported nightmares.

The intrusiveness of these memories has a "here and now" quality. You may not realize the event is from the past. During a flashback, you experience the same physiological reactions linked to a real threat. There are changes in breathing, heart rate, and blood pressure (Ehlers, 2015).

## FLASHBACKS

Flashbacks are a type of intrusive memory associated with dissociation. They cause a loss of connection to your thoughts and sense of self. Unlike typical memories, flashbacks can take over your reality, making you feel genuinely back in the traumatic moment.

The hippocampus is the part of the brain that is thought to be responsible for emotion and memory. In those with PTSD, the size of the hippocampus is smaller. This causes memory to be improperly processed, leading to flashbacks and other intrusive thoughts (Bird & Burgess, 2008).

When faced with danger, the brain produces adrenal hormones that generate various stress reactions. These reactions are described as the "flight or fight" response, alerting the senses. In PTSD, victims experience a continuous production of elevated levels of flight or fight hormones, even when there is no actual present danger (Gillette, 2024).

Sleep is essential to restoration when the mind and body can enter a state of relaxation. But when you experience a traumatic event, sleep patterns can change, getting in the way of this needed rest. These emotionally distressing dreams can happen several times a week or more. Many experts theorize that dreams are a part of the sleep process that helps you store memories and learning experiences (APA, 2013).

The PTSD nightmares can be as terrifying as the original event. They differ from flashbacks, though they share similarities. Unlike flashbacks, nightmares can take any shape or form, and a nightmare may contain only components of the event or overtones of the experience.

Below are self-care practices that can help with intrusive thoughts:

**Mindfulness meditation** can help you learn to observe your thoughts without judgment or becoming emotionally entangled in them. This can help you gain a sense of control over your thoughts and reduce their impact on your emotions.

**Correcting errors in thinking** can help you develop a more positive and realistic outlook. Self-monitoring involves paying attention to your thoughts and identifying triggers that lead to intrusive thoughts. Once you identify these triggers, you can work to avoid them or develop coping strategies to manage them.

**Deep breathing, progressive muscle relaxation**, and **visualization** can help lower anxiety and stress levels. Maintaining a healthy lifestyle can help reduce intrusive thoughts' impact on your daily life. Eating a balanced diet, regular exercise, and enough sleep can help improve your overall well-being. This can help reduce the effect of intrusive thoughts in your daily life.

**Talking** to a therapist or support group can help you develop coping strategies and provide a safe space to discuss your experiences. It can also help you feel less isolated and alone in your struggles (Bilodeau, 2024).

# CHAPTER 6
# AVOIDANCE AND DETACHMENT

## AVOIDANCE

Finkelstein et al. (2022) stated that [A]voidance is when you try to avoid memories of the traumatic event. Avoidance, in the context of PTSD and C-PTSD, refers to a deliberate effort to block distressing thoughts, feelings, or memories related to the traumatic event. If you have experienced trauma, you may have been advised not to think about it, or you may have heard that time heals all wounds. However, going out of your way to avoid thoughts, feelings, and reminders can cause your symptoms to get worse. In its extreme manifestation, avoidance behavior may superficially resemble agoraphobia when the survivor is afraid to leave the house for fear of confronting reminders of the traumatic event.

Consistently steering away from perceived threats may also rewire our brains to perceive non-threatening situations as potentially dangerous. A study examined the impact of avoidance on interpreting social cues unrelated to trauma. Participants with PTSD showed a tendency to avoid even looking at individuals displaying "sad" expressions despite the expressions not inherently signaling a threat (Fleur, 2022).

Below are examples of avoidance behavior:

If you have experienced a sexual assault, you may try to create distance from unpleasant emotions when reminded of the trauma. If you are a combat veteran, you may try to shut down feelings of sadness about a deployment or war zone. You may stop watching the news or using social media because of stories or posts about war or current military events. For example, if you are a hurricane survivor, you may drink alcohol or use substances to try to avoid thoughts or memories of the natural disaster. If you are an assault survivor, you might go out of your way to stay away from the scene of the attack or places that remind you of the assault.

Procrastination is also an example of avoidance behavior. If something we need to accomplish is creating stress, we might avoid it or try to stop thinking about it. The stress piles on if we cannot perform the job well because we need more time. While some people work well with a deadline looming, it generally is the least stressful way to tackle something.

Avoidance coping should be replaced by active coping. This type of coping addresses a problem directly to alleviate stress. The following strategies can help treat avoidance behaviors:

Prolonged exposure therapy involves gradual exposure to trauma-related thoughts, feelings, memories, or situations within a controlled and supportive environment. The goal is to reduce the anxiety and fear associated with triggers by providing a safe space for you to process and integrate your traumatic experiences (Foa et al., 2007).

Mindfulness-based interventions, such as Mindfulness-Based Stress Reduction (MBSR) or Mindfulness-Based Cognitive Therapy (MBCT), can also help you develop an awareness of your thoughts and emotions without judgment. Mindfulness practices can be particularly beneficial in reducing avoidance and increasing emotional regulation.

Art and expressive therapies such as drawing, painting, listening to music, or writing can provide alternative ways to express and process your emotions. These therapies offer non-verbal channels for exploring and communicating complicated feelings, especially ones you may try to avoid (Hofmann & Hay, 2018).

## DETACHMENT OR NUMBING

Almost 15 percent of people with PTSD experience detachment, a lack of connection between their thoughts, memory, and sense of identity. Detachment, while initially a coping mechanism, can hinder healing. You might feel as if your emotions have been muted or turned off. In addition, you may feel detached from people, places, or objects in your environment.

The outward expression of emotions, known as affect, may become noticeably flat or subdued. Facial expressions, tone of voice, and body language may be limited, reflecting a reduced emotional range. If you are in this state, you may find it challenging to connect with others on an emotional level (Beck, 2008).

The dissociative subtype is an extreme form of detachment. It occurs in fifteen percent of trauma survivors and is characterized by a lack of connection between one's thoughts, memory, and sense of identity. You may feel like you're in a dream or a movie or have distortions in time, space, and distance. When unaddressed, it can put you at greater risk for severe mental illnesses.

Practicing grounding techniques can help with symptoms of detachment and derealization. The goal is to help you connect back to the physical world and reconnect your mind to the present.

The following strategies (also suggested for intrusive memories) can help with your symptoms:

Mindfulness meditation helps you observe your thoughts without judgment or becoming emotionally entangled.

This can help you gain a sense of control over your thoughts and reduce their impact on your emotions. Progressive muscle relaxation and visualization can help reduce anxiety and stress levels.

Correcting negative self-talk can help you gain a sense of control. Fixing these errors in thinking can help someone develop a more positive and realistic outlook. This can be done by challenging negative thoughts with evidence that contradicts them.

Sitting on a chair, feet flat on the ground, hands flat on your thighs, and having someone you trust put mild pressure on your shoulders.

Mental games or puzzles, such as counting, reciting something, or having someone you trust describe objects (Van Der Pluym, 2019).

Medications for the treatment of depersonalization and derealization include lamotrigine and naltrexone (Spiegel, 2023; Spiegel, 2019).

## SAMUEL'S STORY

Samuel was a 28-year-old male and a final-year medical student from Nigeria. He had been under severe economic and academic pressure. His younger brother, who paid his bills, had threatened to withdraw his sponsorship. Samuel had been worried he might fail his final qualifying examinations in three months. He subsequently became involved in several religious activities to prevent his perception of impending doom.

Samuel was depressed. He lost all interest in his usual activities and had a poor appetite. He lost weight and preferred being alone. Samuel had been feeling weak, especially in the morning, but had continued with the day's activities. He had suicidal ideation but never attempted suicide. Samuel slept poorly at night because of his nightmares.

I was depressed on a regular basis. Because I hadn't yet received a PTSD diagnosis, I was at a loss to understand my symptoms.

While studying in his room one night, Samuel suddenly saw a complete human skeleton reading at the same table, sitting opposite. At the same time, he claimed he felt uneasy and quite uncomfortable.

He saw the whole room turning, and everything inside became unstable and unreal.

He needed help remembering where he slept that night. Samuel denied all memory of events for the two days from when he left his room to when he realized he was at his brother's house, hours away. The brother reported that Samuel appeared unkempt and looked exhausted but was fully conscious and alert upon his arrival.

Samuel had no history of seizures, manic episodes, schizophrenia, anxiety, or organic disorders. He never drank alcohol or abused any psychoactive substances. He denied a history of head trauma or loss of consciousness in the past.

Samuel presented himself as a well-dressed young man with poor eye contact at his first session. He had poor concentration and impaired vision at the time of his exam.

Samuel took part in CBTs by clinical psychologists, and his depression was treated with paroxetine. After six months, Samuel could write his final qualifying examinations three months later. Samuel could still not recall events from the two days he left school to when he was seen in his brother's house. He reported no further periods of amnesia or wandering away from his place of residence.

CBT helped with my co-dependence, something that hindered our son's sense of well- being.

# CHAPTER 7
# PHYSICAL SYMPTOMS OF PTSD

PTSD and C-PTSD are emotional or psychological conditions that physically affect the body. A somatic symptom disorder is a mental disorder in which you feel involuntary physical symptoms. The mind-body connection is essential to understanding your physical symptoms. Imagine the mind and the body as two halves of a relationship. When they work together for your betterment, the body remains healthy. The body nourishes your mind, while reason maintains your body's functions. The mind can weaken your body's resistance to disease and harmful microorganisms. This happens when stress hormones lower the white blood cell count, causing changes in the body (Kabat-Zinn, 2003).

When we're under stress, cortisol works to shut down certain functions so that our body can focus all its energy on dealing with the stress at hand. Unbalanced hormone levels can cause the problems below:

### SKIN PROBLEMS

Stress can draw water away from your skin's outer layers. Stress can draw water away from your outer layers of skin. When your skin holds less water, it cannot repair and regenerate itself as quickly. This means that even minor cuts or abrasions can leave scars. It can also make your skin feel dry and itchy, leading to acne, rosacea, eczema, and psoriasis (Kiecolt-Glaser & Wilson, 2017).

## SLEEP PROBLEMS

Individuals with PTSD may have difficulty falling asleep or staying asleep due to a constant state of stress and anxiety. This can lead to chronic fatigue, exacerbating symptoms such as pain and muscle tension. This can make it difficult for you to carry out daily activities and affect your quality of life.

## RINGING IN THE EARS

Tinnitus, or ringing in the ears, can be frustrating. Research has shown that when you experience stress, the limbic part of your brain goes into overdrive. Usually, your ears send a stream of nerve impulses to the brain that it interprets as sound. Under stress, your ears can send such an abnormal stream of impulses that your brain interprets them as ringing in the ears (Shulman, 1997).

## HEARING DIFFICULTIES

For many people, PTSD and C-PTSD cause changes in auditory processing, which is the way our brain collects and interprets sound. This can lead to various conditions and symptoms, such as difficulty hearing or understanding what others are saying, feeling that your ears are blocked, or experiencing hearing loss (Marriage & Sheffield, 2017).

## WEIGHT GAIN

Cortisol, the hormone released during times of stress, can significantly impact weight gain and fat storage in your body. Research has shown that high cortisol levels are closely linked to the relocation of fat to the stomach area, also known as visceral fat. This is because fat cells in the stomach have as many as four times as many cortisol receptors as fat cells in other body parts (Kirschbaum & Hellhammer, 2000).

In addition, high cortisol levels can also lead to excessive eating and cravings for sugary and fatty foods, which can further contribute to weight gain. PTSD can disturb the functioning of the hypothalamic-

## DIGESTIVE PROBLEMS

pituitary-adrenal axis and the sympathetic nervous system, which regulate body processes such as metabolism.

When you experience fear or stress, your body releases corticotropin-releasing factor (CRF), which can significantly impact your intestinal function. High cortisol levels can lead to bloating, gas, indigestion, heartburn, acid reflux, and other irritable bowel problems. Excess cortisol can erode the lining of your digestive tract, causing inflammation and inhibiting your stomach from digesting food properly (Taché & Yang, 2018).

## ACHES AND PAINS

Prolonged exposure to high cortisol levels can increase the level of prolactin, a hormone that can make you more sensitive to pain. This means you may experience actual physical pain as a result of your condition. Moreover, the anxiety and hypervigilance that often come with PTSD can also put extra tension on your muscles and joints. You may wake up in the morning with agony in your wrists and ankles due to a wound-up position at night (Riva et al., 2010).

## MUSCLE DEVELOPMENT

Cortisol can have a significant impact on your ability to gain muscle. High cortisol levels can restrict the uptake of amino acids into the muscle cells, making it difficult to grow and recover. This can make it almost impossible to gain muscle—and any muscle gained can be lost in a few days (Philips & van Loon, 2011).

Furthermore, high cortisol levels can lead to overtraining, which creates more stress on your body. This, in turn, leads to more cortisol and adrenaline, which interfere with the release of growth hormones and further reduce muscle growth and recovery. It is a vicious cycle that can be hard to break.

Remembering that your body needs time to recover and repair itself, especially after a workout, is essential. Pushing ourselves too hard can lead to injury and put further stress on stress your body. It is better to be kind to yourselves and your bodies and take any exercise at a sensible pace.

## COLD EXTREMITIES

When your body is in a state of fight, flight, or freeze, it redirects blood flow away from your extremities and toward your larger organs in the torso, such as the heart and lungs. If you have PTSD or C-PTSD, a state of heightened alertness and stress can be constant, leading to chronic poor blood flow to your hands and feet (Van der Kolk, 2014).

## EXCESSIVE YAWNING

Stress causes yawning to increase. Yawning helps cool your brain by increasing oxygen and blood flow when it gets too hot. The quickened breathing that often comes with PTSD and C-PTSD can make the brain think that it is not getting enough air, causing you to take deep inhales or yawn (Gupta & Mittal, 2013).

## ALLERGIES

Your immune system protects your body from harmful pathogens and bacteria. As extra cortisol surges through the bloodstream, it can dull your body's defenses, making you more susceptible to allergies and other sensitivities. It can also cause your skin to become more sensitive, leading to eczema flare-ups or other skin issues (Kelly et al., 2019).

## HEART DISEASE

Cardiovascular morbidity has been noted among veterans with PTSD. A large prospective study demonstrated an association between PTSD symptoms and coronary heart disease. The heightened state of arousal leads to increased physiological responses such as rapid heartbeat, sweating, and hypervigilance (Berwick et al., 2018).

# CHAPTER 8
# COGNITIVE CHANGES

Cognitive changes can vary in intensity and duration among survivors of trauma. The impact on daily functioning may be severe or mild. The symptoms can vary widely among individuals and may fluctuate over time. In addition, cognitive symptoms often interact with other symptoms, such as intrusive memories and thoughts, avoidance behaviors, and arousal symptoms, thus contributing to the complex and multifaceted nature of the disorder.

## ATTENTIONAL DIFFICULTIES

PTSD can lead to difficulties in sustaining attention or focusing on tasks. If you experience hypervigilance, for example, you might constantly scan your environment for potential threats, making concentrating on non-threatening stimuli or tasks challenging.

Altered visual processing may disrupt your attention networks and contribute to attentional difficulties. Future studies are needed to investigate the role of visual processing in attention-related brain function in individuals with PTSD.

## IMPAIRED MEMORY

If you are a trauma survivor, you may find it difficult to remember details of the trauma or even practical aspects of your daily life. You may experience forgetfulness, decreased working memory, and general short-term and long-term memory. Forgetting key appointments, obligations, or responsibilities can cause problems at work, school, or in personal relationships. Forgetfulness can also endanger your safety, such as failing to take crucial safety precautions, following through on accident injuries, or neglecting self-care needs (Samuelson, 2011).

Forgetting critical portions of personal history or life experiences can contribute to a fractured sense of identity and a loss of continuity in your narrative. It can lead to a sense of distance or detachment in relationships when you fail to recall important events or connect emotionally with others (Hanley Center, 2023).

## EXECUTIVE DYSFUNCTION

Executive dysfunction describes a set of cognitive and behavioral difficulties in planning, organizing, and executing everyday tasks. These include mental skills for keeping time, appointments, or deadlines. It may be challenging for you to start or complete assignments. One common characteristic of executive dysfunction is a lack of inhibition or impulse control.

Executive dysfunction isn't a reflection of your intelligence or effort and can be appropriately managed. Most of the brain activity associated with executive functioning occurs in the brain's prefrontal cortex (Barkan & Friedman, 2017).

## COGNITIVE CHANGES

Interventions to improve your executive function include training in working memory and mindfulness programs. Routine structure and organization facilitate task completion and motivation (Diamond, 2024).

## EMOTIONAL DYSREGULATION

Intense and uncontrollable anger, fear, and sadness can lead to cognitive biases, such as catastrophic thinking or overgeneralizing. It was once believed that two different brain regions controlled cognition and emotion; however, recent research suggests they are interlinked. Emotions can help encode memories and receive information in the future, often driving decisions. For example, if a spider bites someone as a child, he might have a mortal fear of spiders (emotion). As an adult, when he sees a spider climbing the wall, his first instinct is to squash it or run to another room (Uttekar, 2021).

# CHAPTER 9
# PTSD AND SELF-DESTRUCTIVE BEHAVIOR

Self-destructive or self-sabotaging behaviors refer to actions that harm an individual physically or emotionally. This behavior has a complex pathology behind it and occurs as a mechanism to alleviate the pain experienced during the trauma.

Tucker and Simpson argue that one study found that 74 percent of veterans, ages 70-80, engage in self-destructive behavior, of which 61.3 percent engage in more than one self-destructive behavior. These can range from isolation to bodily harm. Risky behaviors include drunk driving, hypersexuality, alcohol and drug abuse, making impulsive purchases, gambling, isolation, and neglecting to protect oneself from STDs. Possible consequences include unplanned pregnancies, accidents, permanent disabilities, or jail time (2011).

Cycling through toxic relationships is an example of self-destructive behavior. When there is a lack of compatibility or similar life goals, the relationship may be set to fail. The door is opened to vulnerability with no positive outcome. Epidemiological evidence suggests a close relationship between PTSD and substance use disorders (SUD). As many as 50 to 75 percent of combat veterans with PTSD have drug or alcohol dependencies. Structured interviews detect PTSD in up to 42.5 percent of patients in inpatient substance abuse programs (NC PTSD, 2019).

Patients with comorbid PTSD and SUD have poorer treatment outcomes, with frequent inpatient hospitalizations, worsened physical symptoms, and more interpersonal problems. Clinicians view these dual-diagnosis patients as particularly challenging, in part because they feel uncertain about how best to prioritize and integrate treatment for both disorders.

Passiveness can be considered a destructive symptom. It is caused by learned helplessness from a traumatic event. Low self-esteem can cause you to act out forced incompetence or procrastination because you are too scared to attempt a task for fear of failure.

Another destructive behavior is hyperarousal, where you are kicked into high alert and ready to face a danger that is not present. Consider Brett, a military veteran who walks down a crowded city street. The loud car honking and the rush of hurrying pedestrians trigger his hyperarousal. His eyes anxiously scan for threats in every nook and cranny, never stopping as his surroundings change constantly. The unexpected slam of a car door makes him jump violently. The following night, his hyper-alertness maintains its hold, waking him again and again from a restless sleep. The fatigue from lack of sleep leaves him unable to concentrate on his daily tasks (Sandy, 2021).

Isolation can also be considered a destructive behavior. You can become socially withdrawn when you mistrust other people and your surroundings. If your trauma was caused by domestic violence, meaningful connections, and community support are disrupted.

Self-harm is when you harm your body on purpose. Physical self-harm can be distinguished from suicidal ideation. The behaviors include cutting, punching until the skin bruises, hair-pulling, picking at scabs, nail-biting, burning oneself, headbanging, or breaking bones. Mental health professionals base their diagnosis for self-harm on the Diagnostic and Statistical Manual of Mental Disorders, 5th edition, text revision (DSM-5-TR).

Self-harmers suffer from fear, worry, depression, and aggressive impulses. Links have also been found between self-harm and feelings of numbness or dissociation. Self-harm can be a form of punishing yourself for perceived imperfections or mistakes (Va.gov: Veterans Affairs, 2018). These behaviors may act as a temporary distraction or a way of coping with emotional distress, pain, or discomfort. However, the distraction does not last, and self-destructive behavior can become dangerous.

Many who perform these self-harming acts hide the results. Therefore, it is difficult to identify people with these problems. The most significant danger of self-harm is that you may increase the intensity of your abuse and lead to cause permanent bodily damage.

According to one study, roughly 16 percent of veterans engage in non-suicidal self-injury at some point in their lifetimes, which is approximately three times higher than the rate observed in the general population. Despite being found to be a strong predictor of suicide attempts, this type of self-harm is often overlooked in men, too.

Contrary to common belief, the rates of non-suicidal self-injury are relatively similar between men and women. These behaviors may stem from the veteran's need to seem strong, fearless, and uncomplaining—a mindset that often continues in veterans of both genders well after their military service (Veterans Affairs, 2018).

# CHAPTER 10
# INTERPERSONAL RELATIONSHIPS

## FRIENDSHIPS

Of the people who develop PTSD, five to 10 percent have relationship problems. If you are a survivor of trauma, you may want to withdraw from social activities with friends and family. You may have had trust issues with those you knew before the trauma and lack interest in forming new friendships (Pedersen, 2021).

Numbness, the opposite of emotional dysregulation, can make it harder for you to relate to others. Being oblivious to feelings, spaces, and individuals can cause severe communication issues. Though you may appear to lack emotional depth, you fear that no one can understand you.

Your friends can help by engaging you in honest communication. This requires someone to listen actively without judgment, which can promote the idea that seeking help is not something to be ashamed of but a positive step that can improve your life.

Evidence shows that negative responses to disclosure of trauma (especially sexual assault) can harm a trauma survivor—and that such unsupportive experiences have a far stronger effect than any positive responses to disclosure (Ullman, 1996).

## SPOUSAL ADJUSTMENT

The U.S. Department of Veteran Affairs (2014) reported that approximately 20 percent of service members who served in Vietnam, Iraq, or Afghanistan developed combat-related PTSD.

Mental health issues following combat tours are not exclusive to service members. Spouses of service members affected by combat-related PTSD display symptoms of anxiety, sadness, anger, displacement, and dissatisfaction in the relationship.

According to reviews, PTSD in one partner is consistently associated with secondary trauma in the other partner. A meta-analysis found that although all PTSD symptom clusters were associated with relationship problems, the emotional numbing and avoidance symptoms were most closely linked to family functioning problems and intimacy-related issues. Families deal with ambiguous loss, in which the person with PTSD is either emotionally or physically absent.

Another cluster of symptoms that may affect relationships is hyperarousal. Knowing that a loved one is anxious or on edge can also lead partners to "walk on eggshells" to keep things calm. Further, hyperarousal is the symptom cluster most closely linked to irritability or aggression. Though people with PTSD have never engaged in violence, PTSD is associated with an increased risk of violence (Veterans Affairs, 2014).

Partners must take care of a person with PTSD and take on extra roles and responsibilities—this has been linked, in turn, to partner distress and relationship dissatisfaction (Vogel, 2022).

When partners or other loved ones are involved in treatment, it can be helpful to educate them about PTSD and symptoms, as well as the fact that relationship difficulties are common. Partners can see the symptoms as part of the condition rather than an indication of the loved one's feelings toward them.

When a patient is engaged in cognitive processing therapy (CPT), prolonged exposure (PE), written exposure therapy (WET), or eye movement desensitization or reprocessing (EMDR), clinicians are encouraged to provide relevant family-focused handouts so that the patient's loved ones can better understand the treatment approach.

If your partner has PTSD, it is essential to acknowledge that the past cannot be changed or fixed and, if possible, to focus on moving forward. If your behavior is predictable, it can be easier for your partner to build trust and a secure attachment. Loving someone with any mental health condition can be, at times, overwhelming. Be sure to establish boundaries and practice regular self-care.

Self-care techniques help reduce stress and emotional reactivity, benefitting both partners. Sleeping adequately, eating a balanced diet, practicing creative hobbies, exercising, and meditation can help (Monson & Fredman, 2012).

David Stanislaw, a licensed psychotherapist, gives the following tips for helping marriage partners deal with PTSD. He stressed that PTSD is a complicated condition that can threaten even the most committed relationship. Assure your partner that you'll be there to share and be ready to listen, even if you are disturbed by the events they describe.

You should work with your spouse to identify the sights, sounds, and smells that bring up their traumatic memories. These may be apparent triggers like loud sounds or more subtle ones like the scent of perfume. There are also many internal triggers, such as hunger, sickness, or fatigue. Creating stability at home will help your partner feel safe. Many PTSD survivors are always on guard and feel that the world in not a safe place. Routines create a safe environment, and planning for the future tells your partner that you don't plan on going away.

When your partner is having a flashback, try not to panic. Flashbacks and nightmares are common symptoms of PTSD. However, if you panic when your partner experiences one, it could make the situation worse. Try to remind your spouse to focus on the present.

The prime reason relationships fail is because PTSD can cause outbursts of anger, physical violence, and irritability. If you are the target of your spouse's rage, it is important that you remain calm and avoid escalating the situation. If you are worried about surviving the relationship, calmly suggest seeking treatment with a qualified counselor. Make sure you don't imply something is wrong with your spouse.

## EMPLOYMENT

PTSD can affect your day-to-day life at work. If you cannot accomplish tasks because of panic attacks or sleeplessness, work relationships and productivity suffer. It is crucial to remember that PTSD affects different people in different ways, so a support system that works for one person may not work for everybody.

PTSD becomes even more problematic if you have experienced or witnessed a traumatic event at your place of work. Because one of the primary symptoms of PTSD is the avoidance of places and situations associated with the traumatic event, these employees may have a tough time returning to work (APA, 2013).

Employers should collaborate with you to identify and coordinate the best support system. Once that is done, they must check in regularly with you and provide ongoing support.

The employer can adjust to your needs by taking the following steps:

**Educate yourself and your team.** PTSD can be complicated to understand, so make sure you are well-informed about what it is and how it may affect employees. By improving your understanding of PTSD, you will respond more to your employee's needs. It is also essential to educate the rest of your team about PTSD and how they can support a colleague who is experiencing it.

**Build trust with your employees**. Taking steps to build or maintain that trust is incredibly important. Making supportive adjustments will increase the employees' sense of security and safety.

**Make workplace adjustments**. Even simple adjustments on the employer's part may help you feel more capable of working despite your diagnosis. These adjustments might include allowing you to sit where you feel most comfortable or putting measures in place to help you manage any panic attacks. Employers can promote open conversation around mental health (Vickers, 2015). Often, those experiencing PTSD may find it challenging to open up about it or even admit that they're struggling. This will ensure your office is secure enough for others to discuss their mental health without fear of ramifications or judgment.

## A SPOUSE'S STORY

For three years, I was in a relationship with a man who experienced PTSD symptoms daily. My ex, D., was a decorated combat veteran who served in Afghanistan three times. The toll it took on his soul was heartbreaking.

His flashbacks and dreams of the past drove him to be hypervigilant, fear strangers, and fend off sleep to avoid nightmares. I wanted to take away his pain, but I was also dealing with my own guilt about needing to care for myself, too.

My husband was very patient with my flashbacks and nightmares. He could tell when I was triggered by the faraway look in my eyes. When they occurred, he tried to ground me by talking about the present.

D once described his PTSD to me as a constant waiting game for ghosts to jump from around the corner. It was a reminder that bad things happened and that that feeling might never stop.

We sat outside watching fireworks, and he held my hand until my knuckles turned white. He explained that the only way he could sit through them was to have me next to him. These symptoms made our relationship difficult.

And then there was the skittishness and aggression, which are typical for people with PTSD. I couldn't come up behind him without first giving him a warning, especially when he had headphones on. He also had explosive outbursts of rage, which left me in tears.

My husband was very supportive when I began transcranial magnetic stimulation (TMS). Though it wasn't covered by insurance, he knew it was necessary. I saw improvement after several sessions.

D was the softest, most complimentary man 90 percent of the time. But his cruel side became all-consuming when he felt wounded or scared. He knew what buttons to press—my insecurities and weaknesses—and he had no shame using them as a weapon when he felt angry.

D is beautiful—inside and out. Not only is D strikingly handsome, but he is also intelligent, caring, and compassionate. But he didn't feel he was even remotely lovable.

Her partner had the classic symptoms of PTSD according to the DSM clusters—hypervigilance, negativity syndrome, and detachment. I almost feared my husband would get so impatient with me that he would leave.

D needed a lot of time and attention from me because he had lost so much in his life. He had an almost controlling grip on me, ranging from needing to know every detail of my whereabouts to having meltdowns when plans changed, believing he was unlovable.

D also created scenarios that cast him as such. When he was angry, he'd express it by taking horrific jabs at me. I'd be left feeling torn apart, worried about the next time D would try to hurt me verbally. At the same time, he didn't feel safe opening up to me, another symptom of his PTSD (Vogel, 2022).

# PART THREE
# THERAPEUTIC STEPS FOR RECOVERY

# CHAPTER 11
# THERAPIES

## GROUP THERAPY

After a traumatic event, you begin to think differently about yourself and the world around you. Group therapy is a type of psychotherapy where several people attend the same session. Although 60 percent of Americans will experience trauma in their lifetime, many survivors of trauma feel lonely and isolated from others. Sharing your story with people experiencing similar struggles can be a bonding and healing experience. Group therapy can help you connect with others, learn new coping skills, and find your voice again. Group therapy also offers the benefit of being more affordable than individual therapy. It also provides a place where survivors can access the community and feel a sense of belonging (Pedersen, 2022).

Pederson claims that groups may be aimed at specific types of trauma or symptoms, whether for women with a history of sexual abuse or a group with severe dissociative symptoms (2022).

Group treatment for survivors of trauma has been in practice for several decades now. It was developed around the same time that post-traumatic stress disorder (PTSD) became a formal diagnosis in the third edition of the Diagnostic and Statistical Manual of Mental Disorders in 1980.

Trauma group therapy is considered an effective form of treatment and is commonly offered to survivors of trauma. In fact, one 2017 research suggests that group therapy provides some advantages over individual treatment in that it helps "normalize" trauma symptoms and offers social support to participants.

One 2021 study, Trusted Source, evaluated the effectiveness of an 8-week trauma-focused CBT intervention for female survivors of intimate partner violence (IPV), also known as domestic violence. People who've experienced IPV have high rates of PTSD, anxiety, and depression. IPV is also associated with suicidal thoughts, substance use, and poor health. In this study, the women—all of whom had significant post-traumatic symptoms—were randomly assigned to individual (twenty-five participants) or group (twenty-eight participants) therapy. The study found that group therapy is just as effective as individual therapy. It's also more cost-effective, particularly in the long term (APsyA, 2013).

The types of trauma psychotherapy groups include:

**Cognitive behavioral therapy** (CBT): CBT groups focus on identifying and challenging negative or false thought patterns.

**Interpersonal group therapy** (IPT): IPT groups focus on reducing symptoms by improving personal relationship skills.

**Mind-body skills group therapy**: These groups incorporate mindfulness skills such as meditation, breath work, and guided imagery.

**Feminist-informed group therapy**: These groups help empower and heal female survivors of violence.

**Functional family therapy** for PTSD is a type of therapy designed to help children and their families overcome violence and trauma (Pedersen, 2022).

**CBT for PTSD with a co-occurring mental health condition**: These groups can address both PTSD and other disorders, such as substance use disorder (SUD) (Pedersen, 2022).

## DANIEL'S STORY

Daniel went from being an active-duty marine to taking on unfamiliar responsibilities as a stay-at-home dad. He felt he didn't have any friends or family who understood him. Daniel said that he felt even worse when civilian family members and friends unintentionally put him in the position of asking him about his war experiences. Daniel said he was not the happy-go-lucky person he once was.

He knew that individual therapy involved a one-on-one session between a counselor and a patient. However, he felt that group therapy might be more beneficial for him. At first, he was reluctant to share his personal feelings and challenges with a group of strangers. But eventually, group therapy provided many benefits. The act of sharing and listening to other people's experiences and the feeling of being understood by others was beneficial.

The closest I came to group therapy was the once-a-week prayer sessions with two of my friends. We have done this for 25 years.

Daniel found that group therapy helped relieve the feeling that he was the only one grappling with tough challenges. This realization became the starting point of his recovery. He said that the effects of veterans' group therapy far outlasted the sessions themselves. Expressing his feelings and helping others overcome their difficulties improved his ability to understand others and, ultimately, himself.

## MEDICATION-ASSISTED THERAPY

The three medications recommended to treat PTSD are sertraline (Zoloft) SSRI, paroxetine (Paxil) SSRI, and venlafaxine (Effexor SNRI). It can take a few weeks for someone to notice a change, and a provider can manage the side effects and dosage (AOA, 2017).

To receive medications for PTSD, you will need to meet with a provider who can prescribe these medications. Many different types of providers, including family providers and even some nurses and physician assistants, can prescribe antidepressant medications for PTSD.

The risks of taking SSRIs and SNRIs are mild to moderate side effects such as upset stomachs, headaches, and dizziness. You may have sexual side effects, such as decreased desire to have sex or difficulty having an orgasm. Some side effects are short-term, though others may last as long as you take the medication.

## TRANSCRANIAL MAGNETIC STIMULATION

TMS is a non-invasive, FDA-approved PTSD. The treatment doesn't rely on medication, sedation, or anesthesia.

Various brain regions and their functions are affected in people who have PTSD. Critical brain parts that are affected by trauma include the amygdala, the prefrontal cortex, and the hippocampus. The amygdala is an almond-shaped structure that deals with survival instincts and how you express emotions, especially fear; the ventromedial prefrontal cortex (vmPFC) – is a more sophisticated region of the brain that also processes emotions. The hippocampus is responsible for storing and retrieving your memories (Kolb. 1987).

Brain imaging studies show that PTSD patients have reduced brain activity in the vmPFC and an overactive amygdala. It is believed that the vmPFC loses control of the amygdala, which leads to intense anxiety. The hippocampus shrinks, which helps to distinguish between the past and present. This means PTSD patients find it difficult to tell the difference between past trauma and the present situation (Shin et al., 2006).

Transcranial magnetic therapy works by stimulating the cells in the vmPFC with electromagnetic impulses delivered by an electromagnetic coil. This treatment also helps to regulate cells in other brain regions associated with PTSD, possibly bringing them back to normal levels of activity. Restoring balance and stability in your brain helps ease your symptoms of PTSD. Transcranial magnetic stimulation found that one-third of patients had a significant reduction in their symptoms. The researchers said the positive response is due to increased connectivity between the prefrontal cortex and the amygdala (Deskalakis, 2008).

A double-masked, controlled study published in the American Journal of Psychiatry found that TMS offered relief to patients with PTSD. In separate research with war veterans, 70 percent of participants no longer met the criteria for PTSD after TMS treatment sessions (Philip et al., 2019).

# CHAPTER 12
# CBT AND EMDR

## COGNITIVE BEHAVIORAL THERAPY

The APA strongly recommends CBT for the treatment of PTSD. This treatment eliminates unhelpful thinking, negative thought patterns, and other cognitive distortions. Changing these patterns involves learning to recognize one's distortions that create problems and then reevaluating them in light of reality. Clients gain a better understanding of the behavior and motivation of others by using problem-solving skills to cope with difficult situations. They learn to develop a greater sense of confidence in their own abilities.

Kendra Cherry, PhD, has detailed some common cognitive distortions CBT can eliminate. They include all-or-nothing thinking, mental filtering, jumping to conclusions, mind reading, overgeneralization, catastrophizing, the fallacy of fairness, emotional reasoning, disqualifying the positive, personalization, labeling, and should statements (Cherry, n.d.). Kendra details the distortions below:

We don't live in a **black-and-white** world, and there are plenty of gray areas within the human experience. However, if you are affected by this distortion, you tend to see situations in terms of extremes. Things are either fantastic or horrible, with no middle ground. This type of thinking impacts your ability to process situations with the nuance and perspective required for a healthy outlook on life.

**Mental filtering** is the tendency to focus only on the negatives of a situation while overlooking the positives. If you are affected by this cognitive distortion, you tend to be pessimistic about your experiences and let the smallest negatives outweigh the positives.

**Jumping to conclusions** is the tendency to make unhelpful assumptions based on little or no evidence. If you have this distortion, you may decide not to pursue a promotion because you believe that coworker is more qualified — even if you have no proof that they are.

**Mind reading** is your attempt to interpret the thoughts and beliefs of others without sufficient evidence. If you have this cognitive distortion, you will assume that others have negative thoughts or feelings about you, even when there is no reason to believe that they are true.

**Overgeneralization** is a cognitive distortion similar to mental filtering. If you have this distortion, you will generalize one negative experience into a pattern that may not exist. For example, if you have had one bad relationship, you will conclude that you will never have a healthy one.

**Catastrophizing** is exaggerating an event's meaning, importance, or likelihood. The classic children's story of Chicken Little, who saw an acorn fall from a tree and concluded that the sky was falling, is an example of how you can't control events and emotions.

The world isn't always a fair place — many people learn this at an early age. If you have this distortion, you will be bitter about your trauma because life should be fair.

**Emotional reasoning** is one of the most common cognitive distortions people fall prey to. If you have this cognitive distortion, you will place too much trust in your emotions, leading to false beliefs.

**Personalization** is the tendency to take everything personally and blame yourself for every negative situation or outcome. If you have this cognitive distortion, you will take every negative outcome in your life as a symptom of your own failure — even when there is no logical reason to blame yourself.

**Labeling** is an overgeneralization that causes you to label yourself or others based on a single experience. If you have this cognitive distortion, you will label yourself as unintelligent when you fail a test. This label can cause you to unfairly place yourself and others in boxes that can be difficult to escape.

The tendency to make "should" statements is a cognitive distortion that causes you to hold yourself to too high of a standard regarding what you "should" or "must" do. If you have this cognitive distortion, you feel guilt or failure when your expectations aren't met.

**Prolonged Exposure** (PE) is a specific type of CBT. PE teaches you to face your fears. By talking about the details of the trauma and confronting safe situations that you have been avoiding, you can decrease your PTSD symptoms and regain more control of your life (Veterans Affairs, 2018).

Barbara Olasove, Ph.D., lists the following stages of CBT or PE below (Olasove, 2006):

In the first session, you will learn a **breathing technique** to help manage your anxiety. In your second session, you will work with your therapist to make a list of people, places, or activities that you have stayed away from since your trauma. Throughout therapy, you will work through your list step-by-step, practicing in vivo exposure—meaning you will gradually confront these situations.

Around the third session, you will start talking about your trauma. Your therapist will guide you through it and keep track of your anxiety level as you speak. With time, you will likely find that you can feel comfortable in these situations and will no longer need to avoid them (APA, 2017).

You can avoid feeling overwhelmed or discouraged by tackling your goals and milestones one at a time. The approach is sometimes called "successive approximation," wherein you gradually come closer to your desired healthy behavior with each small goal (Messina, 2021).

The risks of doing PE include moderate discomfort when talking about your memories. These feelings are usually brief, and people tend to feel better as they keep doing PE. Most people who complete PE find that the benefits outweigh any initial discomfort (Foa, 2007).

Progressive muscle relaxation (PMR) is a technique designed to relieve muscle tension caused by stress and anxiety.

Identifying and reframing negative thoughts requires self-awareness. You will need to identify harmful thoughts. When they arise, you can call upon your positive affirmations.

# EMDR

Dr. Francine Shapiro developed eye movement desensitization and reprocessing (EMDR) in the 1980s. She created it as a technique to help people overcome psychological trauma and PTSD. Dr. Shapiro theorized that disturbing memories continue to cause distress because the brain does not adequately process these memories. These unprocessed memories are believed to contain the emotions, thoughts, and physical sensations during the event. EMDR therapy focuses directly on the memory and targets how it is stored in the brain, allowing the memory to be processed more fully (Shapiro, 2017).

During EMDR, the client is asked to recall a painful memory. At the same time, they are exposed to eye stimulation and sound, so parts of your brain work simultaneously. Doing this forces your brain to divide its resources between processing visual information and working memory. Eye movement is a bilateral ocular oscillation that helps reduce the emotional charge of memory and reprocess how it's stored in the mind and body (Pagani et al., 2013).

EMDR induces a fundamental change in your brain circuitry similar to what happens in rapid eye movement (REM) sleep that allows you to more effectively process and incorporate traumatic memories into general association networks in the brain. This helps the individual integrate and understand the memories within the larger context of their life experience (Stickgold, 2023).

The counselors at Greenwood Counseling Center recommend the following steps before undergoing EMDR.

## HISTORY AND TREATMENT PLANNING

Throughout one or two sessions, the therapist learns about your history of trauma. The counselor then designs a plan of action.

**Preparation**: Depending on you, this phase can last between one and four sessions. Therapists teach you a few tools to help you deal with the cognitive disturbances that the trauma caused. The counselor also builds trust with you during this time.

**Assessment**: Counselors use the Subjective Units of Disturbance (SUD) scale to determine how you feel about yourself and the traumas you endured.

**Body Scan**: Therapists bring up negative feelings once again and ask you to identify any tension or physical symptoms.

**Closure**: Professionals check on you to ensure you feel better than when you started the appointment and give you things to work on before the next meeting. This stage always ends the session.

Generally, you will experience fewer side effects than if you were to take medication. However, you may experience emotional discomfort during the sessions. This is typical of any psychotherapy because just recalling a trauma can bring up negative feelings. Over time, you will have fewer reactions to these (Psychology Today, 2024).

## BRIAN'S STORY

A commander had heard that a couple of the villagers had helped out Western forces and wanted to teach the village a lesson. Brian saw enough horror that day to last a lifetime.

He saw the dead body of a loved one, mutilated but still live people, such as one tortured little girl; houses razed to the ground and thick, acrid smoke everywhere. In this case, we did all the "right things" in the village.

When Brian's unit was returning to base, they hit a bump. The IED [improvised explosive device, or bomb] went off, throwing five of them down. Brian lost consciousness, with shrapnel impact to his face and neck. Though he couldn't remember anything about the accident, he experienced confusion, terrible headaches, and vertigo for several days. Brian was diagnosed with traumatic brain injury (TBI). He had no cognitive impairment or perceptual loss, with the exception of some hearing loss in his right ear.

When Brian returned home, he couldn't get the images from the village out of his mind, especially the little girl whose arms had been cut off deliberately. During his flashbacks, he felt like he was right back at the scene again. At night, he had unbearable nightmares and felt on edge, unable to relax, and hopeless about his future. He avoided any thoughts or activities that vaguely reminded him of the ordeal. Despite the avoidance, Brian still felt emotionally numb—just flat. He screamed at his wife and kids for minor offenses. He thought he was losing his mind. Brian acknowledged consuming alcohol up to seven times a week with ten or more drinks per setting. Before his treatment began, he would get drunk every day, often blacking out.

I had nightmares and flashbacks about an incident at our son's new school. He took a visiting teacher's lunch and was expelled for five weeks. My husband and I were upset and went to talk to the headmistress about it. She said that his reputation had followed him to his new school. My knees were weak as I walked to the car. I encouraged my husband to go to school conferences because I couldn't face the teacher.

In **exposure therapy**, Brian learned to tolerate the heightened emotional distress when reminded of the trauma. After extinction was achieved, he showed little or no anxiety in response to the memories. Brian showed a low tolerance for the physiological arousal he was experiencing: a racing heart, shortness of breath, and dizziness. The therapist incorporated interoceptive exposure—finding ways to mimic the symptoms to help Brian de-sensitize from them. This included doing jumping jacks, breathing through coffee straws, and spinning in the therapist's office chair. The therapist explained that, by being willing to have the symptoms induced ahead of time, Brian could habituate them so that they would not be so overpowering.

At the end of 10 sessions, Brian appeared to be much happier and functioning much better in his life. He was feeling more and more "like a new man," with significant decreases in symptoms. He no longer had the urge to drink alcohol and was able to sleep through the night.

## HARRY'S STORY

After surviving a house fire, Harry thought the worst was over—but he discovered that it was only the beginning. For months, he could not get the images out of his mind. He felt like the fire was happening again and again. Harry wanted to get his life back, but the flashbacks and nightmares wouldn't stop. He often woke up screaming and crying. Harry experienced terrifying bodily sensations, such as feeling heat from the fire, the smell of burning, choking, and being unable to breathe. He was convinced he was going mad.

Harry sought a trauma therapist who could help him revisit the trauma in a safe space. He utilized EMDR for over a year. At first, he found it depressing. He wondered whether he had the strength to climb out and face reality. He knew he had to face his memories.

I was treated with EMDR for several years. At first, the sessions left me agitated. With time, I saw tremendous progress. I continued writing, SE, and CBT for a year with great results. Therapy became more manageable after a few months. Harry could pull himself up the sides of the well to see a soft light. Ultimately, Harry became a more positive, sensitive person. Continuing to live in the light, Harry no longer takes his life for granted (Rosen & Lilenfeld, 2016).

It took time for me to find the right therapist. I mentioned earlier that most psychologists are reticent about providing a PTSD diagnosis. In an upcoming chapter, I offer suggestions on how to deal with a doctor who refuses to acknowledge your symptoms.

## JILL'S STORY

Jill, a 32-year-old Afghanistan war veteran, had been experiencing PTSD symptoms for more than five years. She consistently avoided thoughts and images related to witnessing her fellow service members being hit by an IED while driving a combat supply truck. Over the years, Jill became increasingly depressed and began using alcohol on a daily basis to help assuage her PTSD symptoms.

I am to blame for a certain family dynamic that contributed to our son's problems. CBT didn't help me with my guilt, but my spiritual walk did.

She had difficulties in her employment, missing many days of work, and she reported feeling disconnected and numb around her husband and children. In addition to a range of other PTSD symptoms, Jill had a recurring nightmare of the event in which she was the leader of a convoy, and her lead truck broke down. She waved the second truck forward, the truck that hit the IED, while she and her fellow service members on the first truck worked feverishly to repair it.

After a thorough assessment of her PTSD and comorbid symptoms, psychoeducation about PTSD symptoms, and a rationale for using trauma-focused cognitive interventions, Jill received ten sessions of cognitive therapy for PTSD. She was first assigned cognitive worksheets to begin self-monitoring events, her thoughts about these events, and consequent feelings. These worksheets were used to sensitize Jill to the types of cognitions she was having about current-day events and her appraisals about the explosion. For example, one of the thoughts she recorded related to the explosion was, "I should have had them wait and not had them go on." She recorded her feelings of guilt. Jill's therapist used this worksheet as a starting point for engaging.

## JOHN'S STORY

John was a 32-year-old flight medic who had completed two tours in Iraq. He had been discharged from the Army due to his PTSD. He was divorced with a 2-year-old son. The Army psychologist recommended EMDR therapy. He received treatment twice a day for five successive days.

When John arrived for therapy, the first session reviewed his history and prepared him for EMDR treatment. The preparation phase provided John with a technique to use to access a positive state of safety and calm. This helped ensure confidence and control, if needed, during and in between sessions.

John identified ten distressing target events related to his service as a combat medic. He also described a childhood incident that occurred when his father informed Mike (age 7) that he was moving away, separating from his mother, and that Mike would now be the man of the house responsible for his mother. All of these memories were directly addressed in subsequent sessions. I benefited from EMDR early in my treatment phase. I did it every week for three months, and it changed my life—no flashbacks or nightmares.

During the seventh session, John addressed his memory of a mass casualty incident. During this incident, Mike and his fellow medic, Sid, had rescued two soldiers who had been badly injured when their Humvee struck an IED.

During EMDR therapy, John spontaneously accessed related information, and the new material linked up with the disturbing memory, transforming it. In one session, John recalled details about the incident, putting into perspective the severe injuries of the soldier and what he could realistically do and not do. He remembered his determination to save the soldier at all costs. He remembers positive memories of his colleague, Sid, and other aspects of his experience in the army and as a medic in Iraq, saving many lives.

The treatment addressed the belief instilled by his father that he was to be responsible for the well-being of others. While training to be an Army medic at Ft. Sam Houston, John was taught that if he didn't do his job, people would die. John unconsciously reversed that, meaning that if people died, it meant he didn't do his job. By the end of the session, Mike had realized that the soldier's death was not his fault and that he could let go of the burden of responsibility. The session also changed his feelings about what had occurred. Instead of feeling shame and guilt, he believed that he could carry the memory with pride (Beck, 2011).

## YOU HAVE BEEN THROUGH DARKNESS AND CAN NOW SEE THE LIGHT—NOT EVERYONE HAS

*"Perhaps the butterfly is proof that you can go through a great deal of darkness yet become something beautiful."*

*Unknown*

Nobody can understand the true depth of darkness that comes with PTSD. It's your own experiences and your own suffering that take you to rock bottom and then to take those first steps to recovery. You may have only taken those first few steps but you are on your way. Call it beautiful, call it empowered, but the great darkness is now behind you.

It's not a transformation that happens overnight. It requires time and effort but above all, your patience. If there is one thing to take great pride in it's your newfound skills in emotional regulation. There are people in the world who haven't been through traumatic experiences and can't regulate their emotions. How much freer do you feel knowing you have better control of your emotions and thoughts as well as the physical symptoms of PTSD?

The sad truth is that there are so many people who are still stuck in the darkest of their days. They have no place to turn and much like you just a while ago, they feel that there is no solution for them.

Whether they are a parent who lost a child, a victim of war, or a witness of abuse, trauma is a ruinous parasite that eats away at all that is joyous in a person's life. Nobody should live with this and you are proof that it's not the only way.

As the weight of PTSD begins to lift off your shoulders, there is a way you can help others who are trying to surpass their own traumatic experiences and it doesn't mean you have to sacrifice any progress you have made. In fact, one small act to help another could actually help you on your own journey.

**PTSD is hard, if not impossible to talk about because of social stigma. By sharing your opinions on Amazon, others who are struggling with the same condition can see that there is no shame in talking about their experiences and that there are actionable steps for them to overcome their pasts.**

Real words from real people are what can break mental health and PTSD stigma. Your opinions are an invaluable source of information for those who are hoping to turn despair into a meaningful life—even if we can do this for one person at a time. Thank you so much in advance!

https://www.amazon.com/review/create-review/?asin=B0CZJFV95L

**HE SEVEN EARLY WARNING SIGN**

# CHAPTER 13
# SOMATIC EXPERIENCING AND RTM THERAPY

## SOMATIC EXPERIENCING

Somatic experiencing, or S.E., is a form of therapy developed by Peter Levine, Ph.D., to help survivors of trauma. Unlike cognitive behavior therapy, which focuses on the mind, bodily therapy incorporates body-oriented modalities such as dance, breathwork, meditation, and visualization (Payne, Levine & Crane, 2015).

Somatic psychotherapy has been used more frequently over the years, as scientific research has shown that, as humans, we store memories and emotions on a cellular level. This means it's not "all in your head"; instead, our bodies also hold data. Your body is reminded of something even when your mind is not.

The S.E. framework uses guided imagery (where the practitioner leads you through imagining a scene while you listen) or interactive guided imagery. Though much of this therapy consists of reporting one's internal experiences, the behavior part of Levine's model involves the therapist observing behavioral responses, such as body language or posture. By observing and working with the body's responses, S.E. can help you reconnect with your body and release the tension in your muscles, organs, and nervous system.

As a young child, Levine was obsessed with understanding the natural world. His mother described how, as a 10-year-old, he was familiar with Newton and Archimedes. His passion guided him throughout his life, ultimately leading to bodywork and the roots of trauma. Like many, his motivation stemmed from his own childhood trauma.

Levine, the man who changed how psychologists, doctors, and healers understand and treat trauma wounds—shares his journey in an upcoming book, *"An Autobiography of Trauma: A Healing Journey."*

Casting himself as a modern-day Chiron, the wounded healer of Greek mythology, Levine describes, in graphic detail, the violence of his childhood juxtaposed with specific happy memories. He describes how being guided through S.E. allowed him to illuminate and untangle his traumatic wounds. Explaining how he helped thousands of others before resolving his own trauma, he details how his method derived from a study of wild animals, neurobiology, and more than 50 years of clinical observations (Levine, 2010).

Beyond the standard somatic techniques, numerous subgroups use the S.E. framework in the following ways.

**Sensorimotor psychotherapy** is a comprehensive therapy that uses the body as a source of information and intervention targets.

**The Hakomi Method** integrates scientific, psychological, and spiritual sources, focusing on four core concepts: gentleness, nonviolence, compassion, and mindfulness.

**Bioenergetic analysis**: Body-psychotherapy that combines bodily, analytic and relational work based on an understanding of energy, combines bodily, analytic, and relational work based on an understanding of energy.

**Biodynamic psychotherapy** is a combination of allopathic (medical) and holistic therapy modalities that include physical massage by the practitioner.

**Brainspotting** is a therapy that incorporates eye positioning to retrain emotional reactions.

A 2017 randomized controlled trial — the first the review's authors were aware of — followed 63 participants with PTSD. Of the 63 participants, 30 remained on a waitlist, while 33 participated in S.E. No significant differences between the two groups were reported at the beginning of the study. After S.E., however, PTSD symptoms and depression decreased significantly in the S.E. group.

S.E. techniques were used to treat the secondary trauma effects of those impacted by Hurricane Katrina (Jordan & Tucker, 2007). It was found that these techniques had a significant effect. The study was implemented with a non-random sample of 142 social service workers who were survivors of Hurricanes Katrina and Rita in New Orleans and Baton Rouge, Louisiana, two to three months after the disasters.

A study that compared the effects of psychodynamic group therapy (aka talk therapy) and body awareness group therapy for women diagnosed with personality disorders found a more significant change in the group that received body awareness group therapy. Furthermore, the results of the group that received body awareness therapy continued and "remained stable" more than two years later.

In a randomized controlled trial, 44 percent of the participants no longer met the criteria for the diagnosis. Another study examined the efficacy of somatic experiencing interventions following a 2004 tsunami in India. While there was no control group, 90 percent of the 150 participants in the study reported either no symptoms or a reduction in symptoms at an eight-month follow-up interval (Gould, 2023).

Dr. Peter Levine and Dr. Pat Ogden (founder of Sensorimotor Psychotherapy) have researched, introduced, and trained many therapists in somatic approaches, utilizing an integrative whole-body approach to psychotherapy (Pedersen, 2021). They established the ten steps described below:

1. **Developing Somatic Awareness**

In somatic therapy, we educate you about body awareness and how to cultivate body awareness in and around your body. This is a prerequisite for creating change on a cellular level. We begin by identifying areas of tension and constriction, as well as thoughts, feelings, and behaviors that promote a sense of calm and safety. We may practice something small, such as softening a "hunched" back to a more straightened posture, to begin working toward body alignment. By focusing on and amplifying the sensations in your body, you start to deepen your healing experience and allow for change that you can "feel" in your skin.

## 2. Resourcing

This is how we strengthen your sense of stability and safety. In sessions, before beginning more profound work, we identify the resources you may have. Often, we will look at significant people, relationships, ego strengths, experiences, times, and places that strengthen a sense of safety and choice. Sometimes, this creates a "secure space" - a real or imaginary image.

## 3. Grounding in the 'Here and Now'

Grounding refers to your ability to experience your whole self as connected and embodied. The concept of grounding is at the root of mind-body-focused interventions. Alexander Lowen, a developer of bioenergetics, introduced grounding as a concept in which we can live life, fully experiencing ourselves and being connected to the world around us.

## 4. Using Descriptive Language

Today's somatic-focused therapy approach is all about getting curious, getting descriptive, and staying close to the experience happening in and around your body. Tension, anxiety, and trauma memories get processed as long as you can track, contact, describe, and allow the experience to move through you. For example, you're angry at something that's happened but don't want to stay angry and irritated. You can get descriptive to meet your body's experience and help yourself to move.

You may feel feelings of rage well up in your chest. However, as you stay with the sensations and follow what happens next, you'll notice how the anger moves and how it slowly shifts as you focus on the descriptive body sensation instead of the details of the upsetting event. You can use descriptive language to deepen whatever you're experiencing. Some descriptive words are warmth, cold, tingly, sharp sensation, numbness, dull pressure, ease, spinning, lifting, swirling, or calming.

### 5. Movement

Movement is a natural way for the body to navigate through difficult experiences, insecurities, past traumas, and intense emotions. Movement is also a natural way to help strengthen your abilities to show up, be connected to others, and feel more confident. If you take some time, you'll notice how we carry stories and beliefs that impact how we interact with others and the people around us. Our gestures, postures, voice volume, and presence in the room communicate what we believe about ourselves, what we expect, or what we've experienced.

### 6. Co-regulation and self-regulation

Co-regulation refers to how you calm yourself down when connecting with someone else. In attachment-focused therapies, the therapist uses themselves to utilize mirror neurons to help you calm down. Stressed or disconnected clients calm down more effectively. We can better regulate our emotions when connected to another person's sense of warmth, care, and stability.

Self-regulation is when we develop our own tools to calm ourselves down. We all need a combination of both — soothing from others and our own abilities to self-regulate when required. Self-regulation tools are taught to help you move through emotions, and co-regulation techniques are used in the therapy room. They also teach you how to utilize close relationships to help you regulate.

### 7. **Titration and pendulation**

Trauma, panic, fear, terror, anger, frustration, and depression are all expressed via sensations in the body. We can feel overheated, trapped, frozen, disconnected, or lost. Those kinds of experiences and emotions won't move when you dive into them head-first, as you run the risk of flooding yourself and re-traumatizing your mind and body.

When we approach healing from a body-centered perspective, we do so with appropriate pacing and tracking so that the body can tolerate the discomfort and adequately release the emotions that need to be released. Two common words used regarding pacing and tracking are titration and pendulation.

Titration is a process in which we experience small levels of distress at a time, focusing on releasing and "discharging" the tension from the body. Pendulation is used to achieve titration. When you pendulate, you focus on something stressful and peaceful simultaneously.

You may focus on a stressful sensation when processing something important. You then slowly oscillate to a resource, such as trust in a relationship or a reassuring belief. Oscillating through the two helps the body slowly tap into and then release at a balanced pace.

### 8. Act of triumph

An act of triumph refers to a trauma or event where the body needed to engage in an act of defense or protection but didn't. An act of triumph may be to push against a pillow or a wall, feel the strength in your arms, be able to set a boundary or say "no" to whatever it is that you need to stop at some point in the past. Still, it couldn't because you didn't have the strength; it would have been dangerous, or you didn't know how.

### 9. Sequencing

Sequencing is the process by which body-based tension begins to release. It typically starts with a movement, a sensation that moves up or down a part of the body, or an emotion that intensifies and then slowly starts to lessen. It's like a linking experience, where there are a few dominoes, and once the process begins, the rest of the body continues to sequence. Tension in the belly may begin moving upward to your upper body, feel like tightness in your chest, and then feel like your arms are heavy. Sequencing often also brings other forms of release; you may cry to release the emotions and sadness you've been holding.

**10. Boundary setting**

Boundaries are a foundational piece of work when it comes to healing. When you lean into bodily boundaries, you will notice what boundaries you set, verbally or nonverbally. When you lean into boundaries from a bodily standpoint, you will see what kind of boundaries you naturally set, verbally and nonverbally. In the session, you may practice saying words like "Yes," "No," or "Stop" to express limits. Setting boundaries is one of the best ways to feel safe and secure in your skin. Setting boundaries is one of the surest ways to feel protected and steady in your skin and day-to-day interactions (Van der Kolk, 2014).

The following case studies illustrate the effectiveness of somatic therapy.

Sexual Abuse and C-PTSD

An autistic client with a 15-year history of early childhood sexual abuse and developmental trauma presented with C-PTSD. In the first year of weekly Somatic Experiencing® sessions, the psychologist focused on stabilizing the nervous system by gently discharging its activation and allowing it to settle and reorient. Grounding tools were taught to the client to facilitate self-regulation between sessions.

In the second year, the therapist focused on enhancing the nervous system's capacity and resilience by engaging with sensation and imagery channels that were beginning to resurface. This involved gently addressing the peripheral charge from flashbacks and repairing the nervous system by fostering a new sense of autonomy, boundaries, meaning, and connection.

## WORKPLACE BULLYING

A client underwent a back-to-back Somatic Experiencing® session followed by an acupressure session the next day. On the first day, the therapist established new boundaries through an S.E. lens and empowered the client using movement, sensation, and voice. This enabled the client to discharge the activation caused by workplace bullying, providing their nervous system with a sense of completion and repair. The following day, the client returned for another S.E. session to combine the cognitive knowledge of the new story with somatic awareness, creating new pathways for resolving the incident and synthesizing a new paradigm of being.

## DEVELOPMENTAL TRAUMA

A client with early childhood emotional and physical neglect, now facing chronic autoimmune disorders, began S.E. sessions to build capacity for grounding and stabilization. The therapist achieved this through boundary exercises and completing defensive orienting mechanisms.

For example, the client explored their physical boundary perimeter using movement and imagery while we observed nervous system responses. The client then completed the defensive reaction by expressing it through gestures and words, such as a "no" gesture. We also incorporated slow micro-movements with resistance to release anger and frustration, helping the client regain autonomy and agency.

In the second year, we continued to build somatic resources for nervous system regulation through competent protectors or allies, imagery, and S.E. Touch. S.E. Touch involved gradual and titrated touch to notice activation and settling cycles, aiding in healing attachment wounds, particularly regarding abandonment.

## RELEASING RAGE

A client who experienced a traumatic event five years ago continued to feel rage in their body despite various therapies. The client no longer felt angry cognitively but experienced intense physical sensations of rage. Presenting as red-hot energy in the chest, we worked with these sensations by having the client focus on the periphery of the anger and then shift attention to a neutral part of the body.

This concept of pendulation, moving between neutral and activating sensations, was developed until the activation subsided, transitioning into grief and acceptance. The therapist incorporated an image resource and worked with arising bodily sensations, allowing tingling and discharge through the extremities and new meanings to emerge as the body reorganized. The session concluded with 30 minutes of S.E. Touch to release the jaw and rebalance the body for integration.

## RECONSOLIDATION OF TRAUMATIC MEMORIES

Reconsolidation of traumatic memories (RTM) is a valuable resource in helping people manage their symptoms and recover from trauma. RTM is a trauma-focused therapy that does not involve cognitive behavioral techniques. Instead, it employs exposure to the trauma memory at brief intervals to reduce PTSD symptoms.

RTM uses recently improved to focus on updating long-term memories. The process aims to make the original memory less noticeable and then include those changes in the main memory structure. Adding new information that contradicts an essential element of the original memory is called reconsolidation, a mechanism that updates long-term memory. This method can change memory's emotional tone and salience, leading to quicker and greater responses than traditional exposure therapies (Kozlowska, 2015).

RTM protocol therapy is a three- or four-step method that helps the individual to process and make sense of their traumatic memories. Reconsolidation happens when the brain revisits and re-evaluates a traumatic memory to try to make sense of it. Extinction is when the individual is exposed to the trauma memory in a safe and controlled setting to help them process and make sense of it.

RTM sessions are usually ninety minutes long. Clinicians help patients visualize images to allow them to process the traumatic memories without experiencing the intense feelings again. Patients remain calm and relaxed during the treatment as they construct images in a safe environment. The treatments can eliminate traumatic nightmares or flashbacks patients may have experienced and directly related emotional problems. After RTM therapy, people can remember past traumatic events without feeling trauma.

## RAY'S STORY

I was impressed by Ray's story, which was reported by Dr. Levine. Ray was an Afghanistan veteran who was literally blown into the air and almost got killed by two IEDs. He woke up two weeks later in a hospital, unable to walk and talk. Ray had a traumatic brain injury and was diagnosed with severe PTSD and Tourette's Syndrome. In addition to this, he had chronic pain. The reason for the Tourette's diagnosis was that he jerked his head to one side. Levine realized this was a protective response, trying to pull his body in and orient himself to where the sound was coming from. Just before the accident, there was a firefight, and his friends were dying. He was reliving the fear, the terror, the boredom, and then the horrific explosion. He was locked in with nowhere to go.

I have never done somatic therapy, but my massage therapist couldn't seem to break up the tension in my shoulders. I required several back-to-back sessions in one week to alleviate the tension.

Levine said that when he first met Ray, he was still in a state of shock. He tried to speak to Ray, who had his head down and locked in defeat and shame. Levine asked Ray what he wanted to achieve in his therapy. Ray explained that he just wanted help dealing with people and being comfortable in crowds. After five sessions of S.E., remarkably, Ray was on his way toward

## KENNETH'S STORY

Kenneth, a seventy-four-year-old Caucasian man diagnosed with PTSD, major depressive disorder, and traumatic brain injury, experienced trauma while serving in the U.S. Army during an earthquake rescue operation fifty-two years prior. Witnessing children falling into a chasm during this event haunted him, causing flashbacks, sleepless nights, and bouts of severe depression.

As an empath—someone who takes on the emotions of others to a fault—I can only imagine what Kenneth went through in witnessing children falling through the earth's fault lines. It helps me to know that God was with each child.

Kenneth received pain relief medication but no psychotropic drugs for his PTSD symptoms. However, through RTM therapy, he gradually gained control over his emotions and traumatic memories. Initially tearful and agitated when discussing the event, after several sessions, he could recall it calmly and with more detail. Visualizing a different outcome, where the events resembled a movie scene with himself as a stuntman, helped him reshape his memory.

At follow-ups, Kenneth showed remarkable improvement. He could recount the event without nightmares or flashbacks, even when exposed to earthquake news. His emotional responses became brief and manageable. His PTSD symptoms decreased significantly, and he was able to reconnect with estranged family members.

## JORGE'S STORY

Jorge, a forty-nine-year-old Hispanic man, served in the U.S. Army for twenty-eight years, stationed in various locations, including Kuwait, Germany, and Iran. He was diagnosed with PTSD and generalized anxiety disorder. Despite taking Cymbalta as prescribed, he found it ineffective in alleviating his symptoms, such as flashbacks, nightmares, and sleep disturbances.

One incident involved an unexpected attack on the airplane he was on by anti-aircraft guns during landing in Iraq. Another involved loading coffins onto a transport for transfer to Baghdad Airport. Particularly distressing was when he had to load the bodies of airmen he knew well. Jorge felt agitated recalling these traumatic memories, with many details eluding him.

I never used RTM as a treatment, but I can relate to it because of the power of prayer. Prayer serves to reframe my worst memories. I know that God has always been with me and will" redeem my trauma.

He underwent three sessions using the RTM protocol, gradually improving his ability to recall and discuss the memories comfortably. By the final session, he could discuss the incidents without discomfort for the first time since they occurred. Jorge showed no signs of heightened physiological arousal while recounting the events.

During a two-week follow-up, Jorge reported experiencing no nightmares or flashbacks. He also noted improved sleep quality, reduced hypervigilance, and a significantly diminished startle response.

## ROBERT'S STORY

Robert, a 60-year-old Vietnam War veteran, met the criteria for PTSD and sought treatment 38 years after the initial traumatic incidents. Struggling with recalling these memories, he endured nearly four decades of nightmares, flashbacks, and guilt stemming from the events.

His case illustrates the efficacy of the RTM protocol in PTSD treatment. Robert recounted two traumatic episodes: one involving an order to assassinate a call girl he had grown close to and the other concerning a mortar hitting the jeep he was in, resulting in the death of his sergeant, a mentor figure.

By the final session, Robert could recount the story without hesitation, redirecting his guilt toward anger at the CIA's directive. Subsequent sessions addressed his second trauma, with Robert ultimately able to recount both incidents without agitation.

## GABRIELLE

I felt guilty for the many years of disassociating from my husband and son. I had no choice but to do so at the time. I had to survive.

Raising a child who is depressed can upset the family dynamic.

At the two-week follow-up, Robert reported a significant shift in his emotional response to the traumas, feeling less guilt and viewing himself with compassion as a young man grappling with overwhelming circumstances. Six months later, he continued to experience positive adjustments, free from flashbacks and nightmares, and noted a substantial improvement in his overall quality of life.

# CHAPTER 14
# MINDFULNESS MEDITATION, YOGA, AND HYPERBARIC OXYGEN THERAPY (HBOT)

## MINDFULNESS MEDITATION

Though the APA recognizes cognitive-based therapies, many are turning to alternative therapies like mindfulness and yoga. A meta-analysis of 18 studies compared the effects of traditional mindfulness-based interventions to those of a randomized control group in reducing the psychological symptoms of traumatic stress and PTSD. This study included data on 1,219 participants. Researchers found that individuals who tried mindfulness-based interventions demonstrated significantly lower levels of PTSD symptoms following treatment than various control groups (Strauss, 2014).

Mindfulness can help you become more present and aware of what you think and feel in the moment. It focuses on remaining aware and accepting your thoughts, feelings, and bodily sensations. The exercises include describing objects around you, utilizing your five senses, creating a safe space in your mind through guided imagery, visualizing your anxiety, and using affirmations (Hofmann, 2010).

Finding the right meditation type can take time, but the benefits make it worthwhile. In guided meditation, an instructor talks you through the process. This is especially helpful for beginners. In unguided meditation, there's no instructor, and you can choose your own pace and methods.

Meditation isn't a one-size-fits-all approach. This is why it is essential to get clear on what you hope to get out of your meditation practice and try different methods until you find the one that meets your needs. Types of meditation include focused breathing, box breathing, anxiety relief, transcendental, and trauma-informed (Bertone, 2021).

Focused breathing entails sitting quietly and concentrating on your breath. Just by watching the breath, it will start to slow, and the pause between the inhales and exhales will become longer and longer. Slow breathing can positively impact your heart, respiratory, and autonomic nervous systems (Solluna by Kimberly Snyder, n.d.)

Box breathing can help when stress takes over, and you need an immediate way to relax your mind and body. The beauty of this type of meditation is that you can do it anytime and anywhere. Its intent is to stimulate the vagus nerve, which helps you lower your heart rate and bring your body out of the fight-or-flight response.

To practice box breathing, follow these steps:

Inhale for four seconds.

Hold your breath for four seconds. Exhale for four seconds.

Hold your breath for four seconds.

Repeat 12 to 15 times or more as needed and take the holds. Those gentle pauses between inhalations and exhalations help cue the nervous system into relaxingeply.

Transcendental Meditation

People with active minds benefit greatly from TM because it's not about avoiding thoughts but transcending them. This involves repeating a mantra and being present with your thoughts and emotions. You can practice TM even while doing the dishes, helping to keep yourself calm.

The Transcendental Meditation (TM) program has demonstrated a broad spectrum of health benefits and has been researched and implemented globally. Two studies have shown that TM can reduce PTSD symptoms in veterans. A meta-analysis of 32 studies consistently showed that TM reduces SNS (sympathetic nervous system) activation. TM practitioners also exhibited lower baseline heart rate, respiratory rate, plasma lactate, and spontaneous skin resistance outside of meditation (Barnes, Rigg, & Williams, 2013).

Anxiety relief meditation can be a simple yet powerful way to reframe your thinking and increase your productivity. Mantra meditation replaces the "I'm not good enough" inner dialogue with "I am enough." This type of meditation can be beneficial if you need to increase your self-love and self-esteem. It allows you to sneak in moments of peace throughout the day—perfect for those with busy schedules or when it's hard to find time to meditate (Kera-Passante, 2024).

To practice anxiety relief meditation, follow these steps:

With eyes still closed, ask yourself: Where in my body am I holding this anxiety? Focus on that part of your body.

In your mind, assign a color, shape, or texture to your anxiety.

Keep the visual in your mind's eye as you focus on breathing.

Focus now on your exhalations. With every breath out, visualize yourself: What do I need in this moment? This is a place to feel your inner guidance rather than think through it.

Stay with the meditative reflection for as long as you need to feel the anxiety leaving your body.

**Loving-kindness meditation** is a practice that is included in mind-fulness-based stress reduction (MBSR) and is sometimes called "metta" meditation. This type of meditation places emphasis on kindness by creating feelings of connectedness. This can increase your positive reactions to people and things around you and satisfaction within relationships. This type of meditation shifts your focus from yourself onto other people (Knose, 2022).

You can mix and match meditations depending on your schedule or what you are going through. For example, try box breathing or nature-inspired meditation if you are traveling. If you want something longer that forces you to go deeper, transcendental meditation might be the way to go.

## YOGA

Van Der Kolk writes that yoga can strengthen your medial prefrontal cortex to monitor bodily sensations, giving you a better ability to self-regulate and gain control of your body (Best-selling trauma research author, n.d.). If you have PTSD or C-PTSD, you might experience alexithymia—the inability to identify what is going on in your body. Yoga can help minimize intrusive memories and other physical symptoms of PTSD and C-PTSD. This can, in turn, reduce emotional arousal and consequent distress (How yoga can help ease PTSD symptoms, n.d.). When practicing different postures, you should notice which muscles are activated in the stretch—this, in turn, can reconnect you to your body. Simply noticing what you feel fosters emotional regulation and helps you understand what is going on inside your body.

## HYPERBARIC OXYGEN THERAPY (HBOT)

Recently, clinical findings have also demonstrated the beneficial effect of Hyperbaric Oxygen Therapy (HBOT) on veterans with treatment-resistant PTSD. Moderation of intrusive symptoms, avoidance, mood and cognitive symptoms, and hyperarousal were correlated with improved brain function and with diffusion tensor imaging-defined structural changes.

Copyright © 2023 Doenyas-Barak, Kutz, Lang, Merzbach, Lev Wiesel, Boussi-Gross and Efrati.

Shai Efrati has been the founder and director of the Sagol Center for Hyperbaric Medicine and Research at Shamir Medical Center. He has spent decades researching the field and giving treatments, turning his HBOT facilities into the largest and most advanced in the world, and treating in eight different chambers, an average of 400 patients daily from 7 a.m. to 10 p.m.

Efrati heads a multidisciplinary team in which a variety of professionals work together on each case.

Recently, he and his team have been providing over 60 two-hour sessions of therapy to soldiers and civilians suffering from post-traumatic stress disorder (PTSD) since Hamas's murderous terror onslaught on October 7 last year, who have not responded to drugs or talk therapy.

The researchers said those who underwent HBOT had a decline in all clinical symptoms of PTSD, alongside improved connectivity in neural networks.

This unique therapeutic protocol affects the biological brain 'wound' associated with PTSD and effectively reduces typical symptoms such as flashbacks, hyper-vigilance, and irritability. We believe that our findings give new hope to millions of PTSD sufferers and their families all over the world." (Judy Siegel Itzkovich,2024)

# CHAPTER 15
# ART THERAPY AND WRITING THERAPY

## ART THERAPY

As previously mentioned, traumatic memories typically exist in our minds and bodies in a state-specific form, meaning they hold the emotional, visual, physiological, and sensory experiences felt during the event. They're essentially undigested memories. Differently, he could even talk about his sexual abuse without panicking (Fabian, 2019). Clients may create collages of images representing internal strengths. They examine feelings and thoughts about trauma by making a mask or drawing a feeling and discussing it. Photographing pleasant objects builds grounding and coping skills. Clients can also tell the story of the trauma by creating a graphic timeline (Fabian, 2019).

While talk therapy has long been used for PTSD treatment, sometimes words can fail to do the job. When you're having a traumatic experience, the part of the brain that controls speech shuts down. So, nonverbal communication — such as art — is critical to understanding what people are going through.

If, as Bessel van der Kolk believes, traumatized people feel unsafe inside their bodies, they must become aware of how their bodies interact with the world around them. Physical self-awareness is the first step in releasing the tyranny of the past (Van der Kolk, 2014).

Art therapy excels at bodywork because clients can manipulate artwork outside of themselves. By externalizing complex pieces of their trauma stories, clients begin to safely access their physical experiences and relearn that their bodies are a safe place. Just as art can bridge feelings and words, it can also be a bridge to feeling grounded in one's body (Malchiodi, 2015).

Girija Kaimal is president-elect of the American Art Therapy Association. She has been connecting vulnerable populations worldwide with the therapeutic properties of creative self-expression (Girija Kaimal, n.d.). Kaimal's work has been funded by various government, academic, and nonprofit organizations, including the U.S. Department of Defense, the U.S. Department of Education, the National Endowment for the Arts, and Oxfam America on arts-based psychosocial support.

Kaimal recently spoke at an International Art Therapy Practice/Research Conference in London. During the early months of the COVID-19 pandemic, media organizations, including The New York Times, NPR, and Fast Company, featured stories on the therapeutic potential of creating art, each citing Kaimal's research. Her article "How Art Can Heal" was published in the July/August 2020 issue of American Scientist.

Kaimal contends that art's ability to flex our imaginations may be one of the reasons why we've been making art since we were cave dwellers. It might have an evolutionary purpose because it helps us navigate problems that might arise in the future. Kaimal's theory builds on an idea developed in the last few years — that our brain is a predictive machine. The brain uses information to predict what we might do next — and, more importantly, what we need to do next to survive and thrive.

Kaimal was once with a student who was severely depressed. She was despairing, and her grades were terrible. She was hopeless. The student took a piece of paper and colored the whole sheet with a thick black marker. Kaimal didn't say anything. She looked at that black sheet of paper, stared at it for some time, and believed it to be dark and bleak.

The student looked around and grabbed some pink sculpting clay. She started making flowers. Then she realized this reminded her of spring. Through that session, the student could imagine possibilities and see a future beyond the moment she was despairing and depressed. This act of imagination is a survival action.

When we expect a reward, parts of the brain get activated to release dopamine, aka the feel-good hormone. When dopamine is released, our blood flow, heart, lung functions, and stress responses improve. Hence, activating our brain's reward system impacts our physiological and psychological well-being. This study found that making art for forty minutes reduced cortisol levels, which helps us feel calm and relaxed and improves our immune response.

Art activities lead to a state of flow. Being in a state of flow enhances motivation, development, and performance. According to Mihaly Csikszentmihalyi, flow is the state of being completely immersed in an activity. In this state, people are fully engaged and focused on what they are doing (Mike Oppland, 2024).

The U.S. Department of Veterans Affairs states that a trained art therapist has the potential to treat PTSD effectively. A trained art therapist will have at least a master's degree in psychotherapy with an additional art therapy credential. Many therapists may advertise that they do art therapy, but only those with certified credentials (ATR or ATR-BC) have gone through the rigorous training essential for PTSD treatment. The Art Therapy Credential Board's "Find a Credentialed Art Therapist" feature can help you find a qualified counselor.

## WRITING THERAPY

Therapeutic journaling is an internal process of using the written word to express the full range of emotions, reactions, and perceptions related to difficult, upsetting, or traumatic life events. This process can also entail writing to ourselves to improve our emotional and physical well-being (McGraw, 2023).

This type of journaling can be achieved by keeping a regular journal to deal with upsetting, stressful, or traumatic life events. An expressive writing protocol developed by Dr. James Pennebaker is the most widely used and researched method utilized in clinical practice. Pennebaker, a professor emeritus of psychology at the University of Texas at Austin, studied the impact of a certain kind of writing on mental health in 1986.

Since then, more than 200 research studies have reported that "emotional writing" can improve people's physical and emotional health. In classic studies, subjects who wrote about personal upheavals for fifteen minutes a day over three or four days visited doctors for health concerns less frequently and reported greater psychological well-being.

Journaling's merits as a medium for introspection and self-expression have been widely acknowledged. Writing is thought to improve communication across areas of the brain responsible for regulating emotions, involving both the left and right hemispheres of the brain. We can better recognize and control our feelings by sharing information across brain regions. Journaling has been shown to improve mental agility and long-term memory.

Attention, language generation, and thought structure are just some of the cognitive processes at play when we put pen to paper. These mental workouts strengthen the brain by opening up new communication channels. Numerous studies have shown that frequent journaling can increase working memory capacity. We can free up some of our brain power and reduce the strain on our working memory by jotting down our thoughts on paper.

Journaling has been shown to improve mental agility and long-term memory.

One of journaling's most intriguing features is how it can foster innovation and problem-solving. When we put pen to paper, we allow our thoughts and ideas to flow freely, giving them form. This unrestrained speech can release our creativity and inspire novel approaches to old challenges.

This writing protocol has been linked to physical and mental health improvements. It has been used in non-clinical populations and consists of asking someone to write about a stressful, traumatic, or emotional experience for three to five sessions over four consecutive days, for fifteen to twenty minutes per session.

According to a 2019 study, a six-week writing intervention increases resilience. It decreases depressive symptoms, perceived stress, and rumination among those reporting trauma in the past year. Thirty-five percent of the participants who began the program with indicators of likely clinical depression ended the program no longer meeting this criterion (King, 2019).

A study by researchers Emily Round, Mark Wetherell, Vicki Elsey, and Michael A. Smith found that a course of "positive expressive writing," meaning writing specifically about intensely positive experiences over three consecutive days, not only reduced "state anxiety" immediately post-writing but also improved work-related well-being and job satisfaction four weeks later. Researchers call for further work on the effects of expressive writing on organizational outcomes, suggesting that writing might even enhance work quality and creativity in the workplace (Round et al., 2016).

Another form of expressive writing is autobiographical writing, in which you reflect on important life events to give them meaning and closure. This type of writing can help you recognize yourself as the author of your experience with a sense of personal agency. It allows you to better reflect on your life path to understand your situation. When the therapist reads your story, it helps you integrate the fragmentary experiences into a coherent narrative. Describing personal experiences in detail facilitates imaginal exposure to traumatic memories.

An additional form of therapeutic writing is gratitude expression exercises. These include writing a gratitude letter to thank someone you have never sincerely thanked. Gratitude journaling involves identifying at least three good things that happened that day.

Many Iraq War veterans have been able to confront their own war-related demons by engaging in the creative process. The war in Vietnam has spawned books, plays, movies, and art about the participants' experiences, helping them process the aftermath of the fierce conflicts. The book "*Born on the Fourth of July*" by Ron Kovic and the movie by the same name is about a Vietnam soldier who went to Vietnam with great idealism and hope but returned home psychologically and physically damaged.

In the introduction to the book, Kovic wrote that he couldn't stop writing and felt more alive than he had ever been. He struggled to leave something of meaning behind, to rise above the ashes and the darkness. His goal was to share openly and intimately the horror of what he had endured.

The Theater of War Project has been therapeutic for many veterans. This project has revived stories of Sophocles about ancient Greek warfare. Sophocles wrote 2,400 years ago when he inventoried the maladies of combat veterans in his plays Philoctetes and Ajax, which recount two Greek soldiers' anguish during the Trojan War.

The diagnosis has changed over the years—shell shock, battle fatigue, combat stress, and now post-traumatic stress disorder—but the consequences have remained constant: anger, isolation, guilt, grief, helplessness, and, at the most extreme, wrecked families and suicide (Mockenhaupt, 2009). Theater director Bryan Doerries and his team of acclaimed actors, which have included renowned performers like Paul Giamatti, Adam Driver, and Jesse Eisenberg, have performed Sophocles' *Ajax* for Marines Dealing with PTSD, Aeschylus' *Prometheus Bound* for Corrections Officers, and

Sophocles' *Women of Trachis* for hospice nurses, among others. In his new book, *The Theater of War*, Doerries recounts how these performances helped audiences confront their traumas (Goldner, 2016).

Sophocles wrote 2,400 years ago when he inventoried the maladies of combat veterans in his plays *Philoctetes* and *Ajax*, which recount two Greek soldiers' anguish during the Trojan War. The Theater of War Project helps trauma survivors realize that for as long as men have fought one another, they have become psychologically damaged. Wartime trauma is timeless. The diagnosis has changed over the years—shell shock, battle fatigue, combat stress, and now post-traumatic stress disorder—but the consequences have remained constant: anger, isolation, guilt, grief, helplessness, and, at the most extreme, wrecked families and suicide (Mockenhaupt, 2009).

## MARIA'S STORY

Maria was only fifteen when a group of men attacked her on the way home from school. They took turns screaming abuse at her, and then they each raped her. Finally, they tried to stab her to death and would almost certainly have succeeded had the police not arrived on the scene. For months after this horrifying event, Maria was not herself.

At night Maria would have terrible dreams of rape and would wake up screaming. She had difficulty walking home from school because her usual route took her past the site of the attack, so she would have to go the long way home.

Of the five DSM symptom clusters, Maria had four—intrusive thoughts, avoidance, dissociation, and emotional dysregulation. By the time I was finally diagnosed with C-PTSD, I had been having flashbacks and nightmares for years.

Maria felt as though her emotions were numbed and as though she had no real future. At home, she was anxious, tense, and easily startled. She felt "dirty" and somehow shamed by the event, and she resolved not to tell close friends about the event in case they, too, rejected her.

The first step in this process was finding someone she could trust. For Maria, it was her art teacher. To Maria's surprise, her art teacher reacted very supportively, seeing her not as soiled but hurt and needing help and comfort.

Although I have never worked with an art therapist, I benefitted from painting landscapes in oil. When I painted, I could transcend the worst of my symptoms. I felt elevated and transported to another realm.

Maria benefited from group therapy. She began to discuss her rape with others who had been sexually assaulted. She learned that feeling dirty or somehow guilty is a widespread experience after rape. She was better able to express her anger towards the men who had raped her. Working with this group also allowed her to begin to reconnect and trust others.

Though not technically group therapy, I benefited from a prayer group that knew the details of my condition. We have met every week for 25 years. I can understand the camaraderie Maria experienced in a group setting. Although my prayer partners had never experienced trauma, by lifting me to God, they stood in my place.

## HANNAH'S STORY

Hannah learned the language of mental health after 20 years in journalism. Yet, for a long time, she was in a dark place, hiding her pain. Outwardly, Hannah gave the impression she was coping. After all, she led the International News Safety Institute. This media safety charity served some of the world's leading news organizations.

Hannah, as a young journalist, was sexually assaulted twice. Both incidents were related to her job. She also endured a long-term abusive relationship with someone she met through work. She also suffered from symptoms of secondary trauma and C-PTSD because of the suffering she had witnessed reporting on multiple disasters.

## GABRIELLE

I can relate to Hannah. I wrote a successful spiritual memoir with a number-one rating in Kindle books. Though I had accomplished my goal, I felt like an imposter. I was experiencing significant pain at a time when others thought I was on top of the world.

Hannah was experiencing flashbacks, depression, anxiety, mood swings, nightmares, and difficulty sleeping. She was triggered by loud sounds: fireworks, drilling, cars backfiring, heavy items falling to the floor, and certain smells as well: raw meat, overripe fruit, drains, body odor, and specific aftershaves. Sometimes, Hannah dreamed of someone she loved being violently attacked. She would awake to sweat-soaked sheets—drained, disconnected, foggy-brained. Hannah struggled to concentrate or remember simple instructions. She felt out of sync as if her world were spinning on a different axis.

As in my case, Hannah's PTSD symptoms took years to surface. Long after my symptoms emerged, my instinct was to blame myself for being flawed or weak. My feelings were consistent with the emotional dysregulation cluster in the DSM.

Fortunately, she connected with a clinician friend who encouraged her to find a therapist. Two months later, she took a two-week respite from work. Because she was the family breadwinner, she couldn't afford to quit. In a few months, Hannah found the words to speak about her sexual assault. She started writing fiction and creative nonfiction to process her experiences, finding catharsis in her personal narrative.

Confiding in a small number of trusted friends and family members made her realize she was not alone. This whole process has helped Hannah to better recognize when others are struggling. It has improved her ability to manage her expectations of herself and others' expectations.

Hannah didn't choose to have C-PTSD, but she is choosing to do something to help others. She wants to speak out publicly to transcend her pain (Storm, 2020).

## JESSICA'S STORY

When Jessica was growing up, she watched people on television enter emergency rooms, inaccurately believing they were suffering from a heart attack. After a full workup was done, the relieved TV doctor pronounced it was only a panic attack. For a long time, she wondered how someone could possibly confuse emotional stress with a blocked artery.

Fast forward two decades later. Jessica was sitting in gridlock traffic on the Brooklyn-Queens Expressway in New York City, her thoughts drifting. Suddenly, Jessica's heart was pounding, and the air inside the car was stifling. Opening the windows didn't help; she gripped the clammy steering wheel tighter. The tips of her toes and fingers were going numb, and she was powerless to stop her fear.

Jessica would continue to have numbness, panic attacks, and feelings of being out of control for the next several years. Through CBT and medication therapy, she was able to manage them.

I had panic attacks every time our son relapsed. I was paralyzed with fear and anxiety and had a racing heartbeat, dizziness, and muscle tension. I felt like I was drowning and couldn't catch my breath. All I wanted to do was crawl into a hole and die. These symptoms fed into my detached state.

Immediately after giving birth to her first son, Jessica's panic and depression returned. The year she became a mother was the darkest year of her life. Jessica told this to no one for several years because, at the time, the well-intentioned people in her life pointed to the baby in her arms as proof that she should be happy.

After my first child was born, I suffered from post-partum depression. My anti-depressant was changed, and I underwent EMDR. I was terrified at the prospect of mothering a son for the rest of my life.

What Jessica wanted to feel and what she felt were grossly mismatched. She mistakenly believed she was an awful mother.

Jessica's symptoms affected her communication with family, friends, and associates. Her doctor finally explained that she had post-partum depression.

I'm ashamed to admit that, at one time, the stigma associated with our son's difficulties kept me from reaching out. I self-isolated. Members of our church community had no knowledge of our predicament. I wanted to preserve their ideal perception of my life.

When Jessica was nine months pregnant with her second baby, she tried to find a children's picture book to explain postpartum depression. Not finding one, she wrote a book, *The Little Blue Rocket Ship: A Story about Postpartum Depression*. It is told by a boy who sees changes in his mom after she has a baby. As the boy explores his feelings and questions, he is reassured by his mom's continued love for him. Blending fiction storytelling with supportive communication strategies, *The Little Blue Rocket Ship* encourages open dialogue about postpartum depression between family members (Mitchell, 2020).

ERIC'S STORY

During the Rwandan civil war, Eric fled from his village to Uganda and stayed in a refugee settlement for ten years. He had frequent intrusive images and nightmares about his past. At age 24, in the camp, he met a Rwandan therapist through an aid organization. The therapist encouraged Eric to overcome avoidance and talk at length about his traumatic past. During six 90-minute sessions, the therapist wrote Eric's descriptions in Kinyarwanda.

I have not engaged in this type of therapy, but writing a memoir, essentially a narrative of my life, may have accomplished the same purpose. No one read it back to me, but I gained a sense of agency that was cathartic.

After providing detailed descriptions, Eric felt some relief. The therapist reread the written narrative to Eric, asking him to listen carefully and to add to and correct it as needed. Afterward, the therapist helped him explore later traumas similarly and continued until he reached the present.

In session 6, the therapist reread Eric's complete narrative and gave him a handwritten copy of the testimony. Eric still felt intense grief and loss around his family's death, but with significant relief, as he could talk about and share these events for the first time in his life. At six months, his symptoms were so reduced that he no longer met the criteria for PTSD. Though Eric could not read, he kept his written testimony in his hut to show it to his children when they were grown.

## BILL TAYLOR'S STORY

Bill Taylor fought in Vietnam for 13 months at the age of 18. After his tour in Vietnam, he returned home as a changed man. However, he said his experience wasn't extraordinary compared to others who fought with him. His symptoms were lurking just under the surface and appeared in full force a year after returning home. He was pushed into an uncontrollable urge to win the perceived battle.

He knew he had a powerful story, but it took him fifty years to publish it. The title is *On Full Automatic: Surviving 13 Months in Vietnam*. Bill always knew that getting his story down on paper would be a great way to explain it to those who have never fought in a war. What he didn't expect was that it would be so cathartic.

Bill said that he was no hero. The guys in his book are his heroes, especially those who gave their lives. His story is theirs, and he found a way to honor them through his writing.

So many veterans came home from war and couldn't talk about it. They kept their experiences bottled up inside, where they could do actual harm. Veterans respond positively to the book because they share many of the same emotions and experiences. The book expresses things so bottled up that they couldn't relate to their family and friends.

When I finished writing my spiritual memoir, I felt lighter and more positive about the future. Some friends congratulated me, but many were unable to relate to my success. It separated me from those who couldn't imagine completing such a daunting task.

His memoir gave people an understanding of war that they had never experienced. It also explained why so many veterans act as they do when returning home. When Bill talked at book clubs, he had some fantastic experiences. As many as twenty people at a time surrounded him with understanding.

Bill's healing did not come immediately. He cried at every tragic story he related. The more Bill edited, the more he experienced healing. Because writing was so therapeutic for him, he encouraged every veteran to write their story. Once it's there, they will have a choice. They can save it and share it with their children or grandchildren, or they can tear it up. Bill believed the important thing was for them to write their story.

But for those guys who can't talk about it for whatever reason, writing can be very therapeutic. I'm not suggesting that everyone write a book, and grammar or spelling shouldn't be a concern. Many guys are like me; they entered the military from high school. But it's about getting your story out on paper (USVM, 2023).

## HUZE'S STORY

Huze was born in 1975 in Greenwood, Mississippi. He had starring roles in high school plays and attended the North Carolina School of the Arts and the University of Louisiana. In 1999, at age 24, he drove to Los Angeles to pursue acting and soon had minor roles on television. Two years later, 9/11 occurred. The next day, he entered the Hollywood Recruiting Station and joined the Iraq war effort.

Huze experienced unimaginable violence in Iraq. Honorably discharged in 2005, he began having debilitating headaches related to war injuries. When he subsequently concluded that the war was unjustified, he found the pain of betrayal and his PTSD even harder to deal with. Huze's anger stemmed from the fact that many civilians lost their lives and were considered collateral damage during the

Shock and Awe bombing campaign. Huze started pouring his heart out in a journal, which became the basis for "The Sandstorm" (King, 2001).

I can relate to Huze. In a moment of clarity, he decided to sign up. I have made decisions like this in the past that did not work out as planned. My idealism broke into a million shards of disillusionment.

Although the play doesn't explicitly address PTSD, the psychological trauma is palpable as the characters recount their experiences, mourn the loss of their brothers, and convey their feelings about the lives they took. While some remain unapologetic, others offer justifications, but most express remorse and guilt - not for their enemies, but specifically for the civilian casualties of war. The tragic reality is that many civilians were used as unwilling human shields by Saddam's regular Iraqi forces or insurgent groups.

*The Sandstorm* premiered in Los Angeles in 2005 at Theatre Asylum and was performed at Metro Stage in the Washington, D.C. area, New York City, as a radio play in Germany, and several other venues, often receiving positive reviews. Huze continued to act in films while advocating for veterans' rights, better access to mental health services, and creative outlets for veterans. He was healing himself through his writing, acting, and anti-war activism, including an appearance with actor Robin Williams (Goldner, 2016).

## JOE DEVERA'S STORY

DeVera moved to the United States from the Philippines at age seven and enjoyed expressing himself through drawing from an early age. He joined the Marine Corps just out of high school in 2001. At age 19, his unit was preparing to invade Iraq, landing there in January 2003. When asked what it felt like to be engaged in fierce combat there, he responded that it was surreal. He couldn't comprehend what was happening and felt like he was in a movie. He spent seven months there, returning in 2007. The second time was even more terrifying for him because he was aware of his mortality.

Home from Iraq, emotionally scarred from his war experiences, DeVera enrolled in Cal State Fullerton's studio art program. At first, he just went to classes and then went directly home. "I had insomnia, and anything would set me off." He also saw a counselor on and off for a few years, discussing his discomfort at being home and his desire to integrate back into society.

In my nightmares, I experienced falling into a deep crevice. I panicked because I couldn't find a way out. I was having an anxiety attack in my dreams.

DeVera received a BFA from Fullerton in 2010 and an MFA from Yale University in 2014. At Yale, he continued using art to understand and transform his traumatic war experiences and began creating assemblage works from found objects and military surplus materials. Joe DeVera's assemblages and installations are quietly philosophical, as is the artist himself. DeVera developed a universal perspective through his military experiences, which commenced at a young age, became an intrinsic part of his persona and artwork, and may have contributed to his quiet resolve.

In 2015, DeVera constructed a large assemblage installation in an abandoned structure in Joshua Tree. The life-size animal-like creatures, carved wood structures, topographical map paintings of government documents, scattered nuts and bolts, and more were assembled in the dusty structure with the desert wind blowing in; they told of an artist who finds solace by working with detritus while allowing the materials to influence his artwork (Goldner, 2016).

Though I didn't use an art therapist, I began painting independently. I watched YouTube videos first, then found an art teacher from a nearby university. Though my medium differed from DeVera's, I understand the place of art in bringing about transcendence.

## SHIGEKO'S STORY

Shigeko grew up in Japan with a father who was a workaholic surgeon and an absentee socialite mother. She was raised by a revolving cast of caregivers. The unstable home environment caused Shigeko's depression and insomnia. She attended a brutally competitive private school in Tokyo that required long, suffocating train commutes. At age 17, she was involuntarily committed to a mental hospital for a psychotic episode. The doctors attributed its cause to parental neglect and family dysfunction.

When Shigeko was twenty-two, she immigrated to America to escape Japan's rigid society. She thrived as her traumatic past seemed to be behind her. Later in life, however, motherhood proved difficult. When her son entered high school, she regressed into a bunker-like mentality with mood swings and childish coping behaviors. Her trauma, projected onto her son, caused flashbacks and horrific memories of her own childhood. She wanted to give her son the love she never received.

Creative writing helped Shigeko overcome her traumatic upbringing. Her memoir, *The Pond Beyond the Forest*, explores the long-term effects of attachment trauma on an adult survivor. From a Japanese and American cross-cultural perspective, she details how hidden attachment wounds can lead to specific mental health concerns.

The Pond Beyond the Forest alternates between her current life as a mother and wife in Seattle and her troubled upbringing in Japan. As she traces her journey, she shares her experience not only as a cautionary tale but also as a message of hope that it is possible to heal from childhood attachment trauma.

I experienced the positive effects of creative writing. It became, for me, a form of transcendence. Resembling prayer, it reached deep into my psyche and spoke to a subconscious part of my soul.

After trips home to Japan to attend her father's funeral, Shigeko began to find a path forward. Understanding her place in the dysfunctional dynamics of her Japanese family caused a newfound determination to heal herself and heal the family friction in Seattle. Understanding family dynamics was critical to Shigeko's healing. I underwent individual therapy for several years to untangle how my worries over our son caused the very thing that I feared most. My family-of-origin issues had caused a cycle of obsessive worrying (Yahuda et al., 2016).

# PART FOUR
# CULTIVATING RESILIENCE AND EMOTIONAL STABILITY

# CHAPTER 16
# DAILY ROUTINES AND NUTRITIONAL HELP

## DAILY ROUTINES

Highly successful individuals emphasize the importance of routines in their daily lives. Every entrepreneur appears to be up before sunrise, drinking coffee, reading a few pages, and visualizing their day. Though you don't need to be up before the rest of the world to have a great life, creating an intentional routine is a good idea.

Individuals striving to overcome mental illness or substance abuse understand the significance of routine. Repetitive routines are calming and help reduce anxiety, giving you more control over your day and life.

You can make routines work for you by completing daily tasks simultaneously and removing as many variables as possible. Too many options, like deciding what to wear or what to eat, can create stress. Decluttering your closet, planning easy weeknight meals, and streamlining your entertainment choices can also help.

If you are in recovery, you must make enough time to attend therapy and meetings. They can provide you with a framework to navigate as you progress throughout the day. It's also essential when the unexpected happens, and life feels chaotic and out of control. Despite what goes on in the world, there's comfort and consistency in routine (NIDA, 2020).

Researchers at Acenda Integrative Health list the following benefits of following routines:

### Starting Your Day Off Right

Determine when to leave the house and set your alarm to handle at-home tasks first. Establish and stick to a routine to save physical energy and mental effort.

### Making Better Decisions

Reserve your mental focus for significant choices like job offers or home purchases.

### Sleeping Better

Maintain a consistent bedtime routine for good sleep hygiene. Turn off electronic devices an hour before bed and avoid stressful conversations. Instead, read something light or meditate. Brush your teeth and wash your face well before bedtime to ensure timely sleep and a refreshed wake-up.

### Enjoying Quality Time with Loved Ones

Even with busy schedules, a weeknight family dinner routine ensures time together. The COVID-19 pandemic has allowed for more regular mealtimes with household members.

### Having More Time for Activities You Love

Efficient routines free up time for enjoyable activities like walks, yoga, gardening, or reading (Kohl, 2021).

### Nutritional Help

Research has shown that people living with PTSD will turn to comfort food to feel better. You may desire processed foods like chips, cakes, biscuits, and ice cream. While the spike in sugar levels in these foods offers a temporary feel-good response, it only lasts briefly. Cravings may happen quite unconsciously, as the actions of cortisol, a stress hormone produced in the adrenal glands, prompt feelings of hunger (Gilles, 2018).

Your GP should check your cortisol levels. Cortisol increases the amount of fat stored in the stomach, resulting in tiredness, difficulty getting up in the mornings, and, conversely, feeling no appetite. Research has shown that meal patterning is vital in helping us regulate our eating, whether that is eating too little or too much due to stress.

When your body undergoes extreme stress, your need for micronutrients increases. While biomarkers such as blood tests can pinpoint deficiencies, there is also a synergistic effect of many vitamins. For example, Vitamin C is essential for good iron absorption. Vitamin D, the "feel good" vitamin, is vital to your well-being. A study of PTSD participants found that 62.7 percent were deficient in Vitamin D (Amirani, 2017).

Reliance on the Western diet of processed foods puts you at risk for magnesium deficiency. Magnesium sufficiency is particularly relevant if you have PTSD: not enough magnesium will increase pro-inflammatory markers in the body. As discussed previously, chronic low-level inflammation is implicated in depression and anxiety. Additionally, magnesium deficiency is linked to a higher prevalence of diabetes and cardiovascular disease (Gilles, 2018).

Following the East Japan earthquake, rescue workers were involved in a random parallel-group trial of fish oil (Alquraan et al., 2019). A study on the gut microbiome of U.S. veterans suffering from high levels of PTSD concluded there were alterations in the gut microbiota. The risk of cardiovascular disease is heightened in those with fewer microbiota populations. The role of the vagus nerve is involved with gut dysbiosis (Gillett, 2024). Additionally, 90 percent of serotonin, a powerful feel-good neurotransmitter, is created in the gut. We rely on good bacteria to help break down our foods, particularly proteins, to produce neurotransmitters.

When your body is stressed for prolonged periods, your blood homocysteine levels can become elevated, causing an increased risk of cardiovascular disease and mental health difficulties. Eating a healthy diet will help boost your B vitamins.

Researchers at the University of North Carolina recommend the following diet to counteract stress: Reduce sugar and processed foods and replace them with more complex carbohydrates, like wholegrain bread, porridge, or brown rice. Eating a low-glycemic load (G.L.) diet by avoiding sugar and refined carbohydrates is helpful. Your diet should include whole grains, seeds, nuts, berries, green leafy vegetables, and salads. Good protein sources are also important, such as lean chicken or fish.

Avoiding fats is unnecessary; eat the good ones, such as those found in avocados, walnuts, or oily fish. Mindful eating could help, too, as it involves slowing down the act of eating and being aware of your food, increasing enjoyment of all the healthy things you are eating.

Eat carrots, onions, leeks, broccoli, oats, garlic, tomatoes, and lentils because they are rich in fiber and contain prebiotics. Ensuring a good fiber supply of fresh vegetables and fruit will help support your gut microbiome. If you decide to take a probiotic, check whether the levels of bacteria provided are significant and whether they are strains that can survive stomach acid.

Eat at least two to three portions of oily fish (such as mackerel, sardines, or salmon) weekly. If you do not eat fish regularly, look for a good-quality fish oil to supplement your omega-3 intake. If you're vegan or vegetarian, alternatives can be found in seaweed, algae, walnuts, linseed, or flaxseed. Medical research links inflammation to numerous chronic diseases and mental conditions like depression, anxiety, and PTSD (Grosso et al., 2014).

The brain's hypothalamic-pituitary-adrenal (HPA) Dana, a survivor of domestic violence, suffered from the debilitating effects of post-traumatic stress disorder (PTSD). She was haunted by the central nervous system's inability to forget the trauma, leading to flashbacks, nightmares, hypervigilance, and the recurrence of emotions experienced during the abuse. Along with Dana's mental struggles, she experienced chronic physical pain. She had constant fatigue, improper muscle healing, and overall body dysfunction. Exercise felt counterproductive, medication led to suicidal thoughts, and while therapy was beneficial, it wasn't enough.

Dana turned to research. Although she knew that medication and therapy were standard treatments, she discovered that nutrition is crucial to mental health. With a history of family loss due to prescription drug abuse, she gravitated towards holistic health. Her research highlighted inflammation as a silent killer linked to PTSD. She was consuming all the foods that caused inflammation. Despite the daunting task of changing lifelong eating habits, the prospect of continuing to live in pain was even scarier. Dana decided to adopt a plant-based diet.

The change was transformative. Despite rigorous exercise, she lost over 30 pounds. Additional vitamins and supplements further enhanced her brain and body function. The battles associated with PTSD rapidly subsided, thanks to reduced inflammation.

I have been on the Keto diet for years. Though it is far from vegetarian, research has shown that this diet may have anti-inflammatory properties that could help with chronic pain and other conditions.

Dana occasionally consumes meat on special occasions and avoids dairy as much as possible. The physical impact of consuming these foods makes it easier to avoid them. It's about finding balance and listening to your body. Dana emphasizes that only you have the power to take control of your mental and physical health. The abuse you endured does not have to define your future. Embrace the changes that bring you healing and live your best life (Rutherford, 2024).

# CHAPTER 17
# SEEKING HELP AND CREATING A SUPPORT NETWORK

## CREATING A SUPPORT NETWORK

It can be difficult to share or talk about PTSD. It can be stressful for you to share your diagnosis, but there are healthy ways to engage in conversations about your trauma.

Misconceptions may prevent you from seeking help and leave you isolated. Mental health disorders have a long-standing history of being stigmatized. People with depression are often labeled as 'lazy' and 'weak,' and those with anxiety disorders are usually seen as 'dramatic,' 'hysterical,' or 'crazy.'

It is helpful to talk to others with PTSD and ask them how they shared their diagnosis with those they love. You might ask when and how they decided to share. What would they do differently if they had to do it again? What worked well for them when they decided to open up about their experience?

## TIPS FOR SUPPORTING SOMEONE WITH PTSD

Helping someone with PTSD can be challenging and overwhelming due to the severe impact it can have on their life. It's important to remember that you, as a friend or loved one, cannot cure their PTSD or force them to seek help. Instead, focus on showing care and encouraging them to seek treatment or online support through teletherapy, though the decision ultimately lies with them. Here are nine ways to assist a loved one with PTSD:

1. Educate Yourself on PTSD: PTSD is often misunderstood and stigmatized. Start by learning about the symptoms and emotional experiences associated with PTSD. This knowledge will help you understand, empathize, and clear up misconceptions.

2. Be supportive: Individuals with PTSD may experience social isolation due to anxiety or fear of judgment. Offer your support by listening and showing that you care without pressuring them to share or take actions they're not ready for. Be a steady, reliable, and trustworthy presence in their life.

3. Be Patient (Don't Pressure Them): Discussing PTSD can be difficult and triggering. Be patient and wait for them to feel comfortable sharing their experiences in their own time and at their own pace. Pushing them to talk before they're ready can be harmful.

4. Active listening is crucial: When the survivor is ready to talk, show that you're engaged without comparing your experiences or feelings. Even if you've experienced PTSD yourself, avoid saying you understand, as their experience is unique. Simply listening is often enough.

5. Don't Judge: People with PTSD may fear they cannot share their experiences without being treated differently.

Show respect for their experiences and feelings. Avoid minimizing their feelings or suggesting that PTSD is a personal failure. Statements like "It could have been worse" can be damaging.

Learn about their triggers. Triggers can be unique to each person and can cause a fear response. Talk to your friend about their specific triggers and help them avoid these triggers whenever possible.

Encourage them to seek treatment. While you can't force someone to seek treatment, you can encourage them if they're ready. Research treatment options and share this information when they are open to it.

Take care of yourself. Supporting someone with PTSD can be taxing. Remember to set boundaries and take care of your own well-being. Develop healthy coping mechanisms and make time for activities that bring you joy.

**SEEKING HELP**

When my doctor refused to acknowledge my symptoms, I searched for and found a new one who directed me to a TMS center nearby. Trust is fundamental in the realm of healthcare. Confiding in doctors when we present our symptoms, medical history, and inquiries, we anticipate solutions or sincere efforts to find them (NAM, 2019).

How do you proceed when your intuition insists something is wrong despite medical professionals telling you otherwise? Perhaps you're told that it's just stress, a minor ailment, or dismissed with the phrase, "It's all in your head." If your healthcare professional doesn't listen to or heed your concerns, the following steps will help you get the answers you need (Davis & Nicholas, 2016).

1. If your symptoms are ignored, ask, "What might this be?" And then ask, "What do I do if these symptoms worsen?" These questions will help the doctor stop and consider the options.

2. Try to find a medical practice you can trust. Healthcare professionals are under severe time constraints, but that doesn't mean they shouldn't have time to hear their patients' reasonable concerns and goals. If you feel your doctor or nurse practitioner consistently ignores what you have to say, even if your symptoms continue progressing, find another primary care practice.

3. If you feel your primary care doctor doesn't take your symptoms seriously, ask for a referral to a specialist or go to a different practice for a second opinion. A fresh set of eyes can be beneficial.

4. Review how to present your symptoms factually, clearly, quickly, and without unnecessary minutiae. Sometimes, symptoms

aren't ignored by the doctor; they're just lost in a list that's too long or includes what the clinician feels are irrelevant details. Ask them how to best present the information. Most importantly, put your symptoms into context.

5. Learn about the screenings that should be performed routinely for patients of your age, gender, and race. If they refuse to do the relevant routine screenings, seek another medical practice that is more conscientious and aware of why different genders, ages, and races have other medical concerns.

6. Distinguishing between delayed diagnoses and dismissed symptoms can be difficult. Delays can be a matter of your doctor asking you to return for another visit if your symptoms persist (Green, 2018).

## LICENSED PRACTITIONERS FOR PTSD

There are many types of professionals who provide evidence-based psychotherapy and medication to people who have experienced trauma. The information below reviews the most common types of licensed mental health providers—called psychiatric care providers—and generally explains their education, training, and services.

Mental health professionals can have different training, credentials, or licenses. Providers can also offer other services based on their expertise. If you are looking for a particular type of treatment (like medications) or expert focus, the license and specialized training of the mental health provider is essential. Your health insurance provider may also allow you to see only certain mental health professionals. Check your policy for details.

### Psychologists

Psychologists have the title of "doctor" because of their doctoral degree, but in most states, they cannot prescribe medicine.

### Clinical Social Workers

Social work aims to enhance human well-being by helping people meet basic human needs. Licensed social workers also focus on diagnosis and treatment and specialize in mental health, aging, and family and children. Most licensed social workers have a master's degree from two years of graduate training (e.g., MSW) or a doctoral degree in social work (e.g., DSW or PhD).

**Licensed Professional Mental Health Counselors**

Mental health professionals who obtain a master's degree in counseling, psychology, or marriage and family therapy may be licensed to provide individual and/or group counseling. These counselors must meet requirements that vary by state. Some examples include Licensed Marriage and Family Therapists (LMFT) and Licensed Professional Counselors (LPC).

**Psychiatrists**

Psychiatrists have a Doctor of Allopathic Medicine (M.D.) or Doctor of Osteopathic Medicine (D.O.) degree and specialized training in diagnosing and treating mental health problems. Since they are medical doctors, psychiatrists can prescribe medicine. Some may also provide psychotherapy.

**Psychiatric Nurses or Nurse Practitioners**

Psychiatric mental health nurses (PMHN) can have different levels of training. Most are registered nurses (RN) with additional training in psychiatry or psychology. Psychiatric mental health advanced practice registered nurses (PMH-APRN) have a graduate degree. In most states, psychiatric nurses and psychiatric nurse practitioners can prescribe medicine.

**The 10 Best Online Trauma Therapy Services of 2024**

- Best for PTSD: Talkspace
- Best for Gender and Sexuality-Based Trauma: Inclusive Therapists Directory
- Best for Couples: SereneTalk
- Best for Psychiatry: Talkiatry
- Best for Family Trauma: Thriveworks
- Best for Persistent Complex Bereavement Disorder: Circles

- Best Directory: Choosing Therapy

**ABOUT FACE** is an educational website that explains PTSD using video stories and easy-to-read text from real veterans, veteran family members, and V.A. treatment providers to help explain the experience of living with PTSD and the benefits of effective PTSD treatment.

The veterans on the site span more than six decades of military experience and give valuable advice about their PTSD symptoms and treatment. Partners, children, and friends talk about what it's like to live with someone who has PTSD. Treatment providers (including social workers, psychologists, and psychiatrists) can explain what PTSD is, answer questions, and describe the best treatment (Veterans Affairs, 2012).

**IMAGINE A WORLD WHERE PTSD WASN'T SOMETHING WE BRUSHED UNDER THE RUG BUT INSTEAD...FOUGHT TOGETHER!**

I commend you for your progress, truly! You have achieved what so many haven't been able to. But perhaps it's not for lack of trying. Maybe they didn't just have the knowledge to do so. Your review could change this and give other PTSD sufferers the guidance they need.

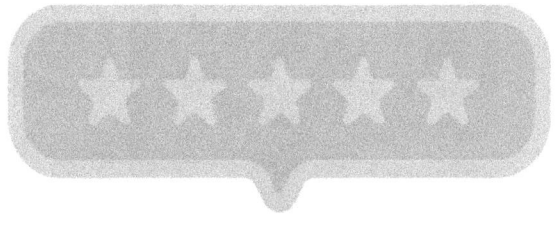

# LET'S HEAR FROM YOU!

I promise it's a simple process, just a few clicks and a couple of minutes and that could be enough to make all the difference. Personally, I can't wait to read your opinions and celebrate your achievements with you. I am grateful that you have shared your experiences and that you have joined me in the fight against mental health stigma. Thank you so much and good luck!

https://www.amazon.com/review/create-review/?asin=B0CZJFV95L

**GABRIELLE**

# CONCLUSION

The goal of this book is to spread awareness about PTSD and the need for early intervention. Despite the growing awareness of PTSD, the symptoms often mimic other psychiatric disorders, causing psychiatrists to have a "wait and see" attitude. Unfortunately, you may go for years without obtaining an accurate diagnosis. If you question whether you have the diagnosis, the early warning signs addressed in this book will serve as reliable indicators. Hopefully, you will use the strategies and resources in this book to gain control of your healing process. Though treatment constantly evolves and looks different for everyone, therapy, and medications can significantly improve your symptoms and functioning.

After utilizing CBT and art therapy, Rose's symptoms were drastically reduced. She has set positive goals for her future. I benefited from using TMS, EMDR, landscape painting, and writing therapy. Today, our son is emotionally healthy, and because of counseling, my husband and I can say, "All's well that ends well." We just celebrated our fiftieth wedding anniversary.

Having spent hours sharing our personal stories and comparing treatment modalities, Rose and I have become lifelong friends. Our journeys should be a beacon of hope for all who fear addressing the seven warning signs. The personal healing stories reflect a variety of therapeutic steps that cater to specific diverse needs. I believe they will encourage you by showing that you are not alone. Writing about the current treatments has encouraged me, giving me greater confidence in the human capacity for resilience. We are all broken at times. We are not perfect people, and we all suffer from trauma of some sort or another. Telling your story can increase public awareness and thereby catalyze the return of hope, dignity, and wholeness.

# REFERENCES

Alquraan, L., Alzoubi, K. H., Hammad, H., Rababa'h, S. Y., & Mayyas, F (2019). Omega-3 fatty acids prevent post-traumatic stress disorder-induced memory impairment. Biomolecules, 9(3), 100. https://doi.org/10.3390/biom9030100

Amirani, E., Pazhiyannur, R. P., & Weiss, D. S (2017). Vitamin D levels in veterans with posttraumatic stress disorder. Journal of Clinical Psychopharmacology, 37(3), 251-256. doi: 10.1097/JCP.0000000000000674

American Psychiatric Association (n.d.). DSM: Psychiatry Online. Retrieved [date you accessed the site], from https://www.psychiatry.org/psychiatrists/practice/dsm

American Psychological Association (2013). Diagnostic and statistical manual of mental disorders (5th ed.). Arlington, VA: American Psychological Association.

American Psychological Association (2020). PTSD medication guidelines. APA. https://www.apa.org/ptsd-guideline/treatments/medications

Barkan, S. E., & Friedman, N. P (2017). Executive Functions: Concept, Theory, and Practice. In J. A. Sergeant (Ed.), Executive Function, Self-Regulation, and Effort Control (pp. 3-38). New York, NY: Routledge.

Barnes, V. A., Rigg, J. L., & Williams, J. J (2013). Clinical case series: treatment of PTSD with transcendental meditation in active duty military personnel. Military medicine, 178(7), e836-e840.

Barry, E (2023) She redefined trauma then trauma redefined her. *The New York Times.* https://www.nytimes.com/2023/04/24/health/judith-herman-trauma.html

Beck, A. T (2008). The evolution of the cognitive model of depression and its neurobiological correlates. *American Journal of Psychiatry*, 165(8), 969-977. doi: 10.1176/appi.ajp.2008.08050741

Beck, A. T (2011). Cognitive Behavior Therapy: Basics and Beyond (2nd ed.). New York: Guilford Press.

Bertone, H.J (2021). Which type of meditation is right for me?, Healthline. https://www.healthline.com/health/mental-health/types-of-meditation

Berwick, D. R., Boyko, E. J., Gardner, J. W., & Keane, T. M (2018). The postdeployment reintegration experience of veterans: A systematic review. Journal of Clinical Psychology, 74(1), 13-34. DOI: 10.1002/jclp.22523

Bilodeau, K (2024). Managing intrusive thoughts, Harvard Health. https://www.health.harvard.edu/mind-and-mood/managing-intrusive-thoughts

Bird, C. M., & Burgess, N (2008). The hippocampus and memory: insights from spatial processing. Nature reviews neuroscience, 9(3), 182-194.

Born on the 4th of July (1989). Directed by Oliver Stone, Universal Pictures.

Bourke, J (2016). Tribe: On homecoming and belonging – Review. The Guardian. https://www.theguardian.com/books/2016/jun/26/tribe-homecoming-belonging-review-sebastian-junger-joanna-bourke

Bride, B. E., Radey, M., & Figley, C. R (2007). Measuring Compassion Fatigue. *Clin Soc Work J, 35*(3), 155–163. https://doi.org/10.1007/s10615-007-0087-3

Canino, G., Bravo, M., Rubio-Stipec, M., & Woodbury, M (1990). The impact of disaster on mental health: Prospective and retrospective analyses. *International Journal of Mental Health, 19*(1), 51-69. doi:10.1080/00207411.1990.11449163

Card, D., & Lemieux, T (2001). Going to College to Avoid the Draft: The Unintended Legacy of the Vietnam War. *The American Economic Review, 91*(2), 97-102.

Cherry, K (n.d.). Cognitive Distortions: What Are Cognitive Distortions? *Verywell Mind*. Retrieved from https://www.verywellmind.com/what-are-cognitive-distortions-4178989

Cloitre, M., Garvert, D. W., Weiss, B., Carlson, E. B., & Bryant, R. A (2014). Distinguishing PTSD, Complex PTSD, and Borderline Personality Disorder: A latent class analysis. *European Journal of Psychotraumatology, 5*(1), 25097. https://doi.org/10.3402/ejpt.v5.25097

Daskalakis, Z. J., Levinson, A. J., & Fitzgerald, P. B (2017). Repetitive transcranial magnetic stimulation (rTMS) for treating post-traumatic stress disorder (PTSD). Expert Review of Neurotherapeutics, 17(3), 231-239. doi: 10.1080/14737175.2017.1283044

Davis, L. L., Schein, J., Cloutier, M., Gagnon-Sanschagrin, P., Maitland, J., Urganus, A., Guerin, A., Lefebvre, P., & Houle, C. R (2020). The economic burden of posttraumatic stress disorder in the United States from a societal perspective. *The Journal of Clinical Psychiatry*, 83(3). https://doi.org/10.4088/jcp.21m14116

Davis, L. L., Schein, J., Cloutier, M., Gagnon-Sanschagrin, P., Maitland, J., Urganus, A., ... & Houle, C. R (2022). The economic burden of posttraumatic stress disorder in the United States from a societal perspective. *The Journal Of Clinical Psychiatry*, 83(3), 40672.

Davis, R. E., & Nicholas, B (2016). Crossing the border: Patient-provider disparities in healthcare provider-patient communication. Patient Education and Counseling, 99(12), 1935-1944. doi: 10.1016/j.pec.2016.07.017

Davis, S (2021). *Self-harm and complex PTSD*. CPTSD foundation.

Diamond, A., (2024). How to sharpen executive functions: Activities to hone brain skills. ADDitude. https://www.additudemag.com/how-to-improve-executive-function-adhd/

Daskalakis, Z. J., Levinson, A. J., & Fitzgerald, P. B (2008). Repetitive transcranial magnetic stimulation for major depressive disorder: A review. Expert Review of Neurotherapeutics, 8(1), 139-147. doi: 10.1586/14737175.8.1.139

Dibdin, E (2022). How does PTSD lead to emotional dysregulation? *Psych Central*. https://psychcentral.com/ptsd/affect-dysregulation-and-c-ptsd

Donadon, M. F., Martin-Santos, R., & Osorio, F. D. L (2018). The associations between oxytocin and trauma in humans: A systematic review. *Frontiers in Pharmacology, 9*, Article 300900.

Edersheim, J. G (n.d.). Staff profile. The Center for Law, Brain & Behavior. Retrieved [July 29, 2024, from https://clbb.mgh.harvard.edu/staff/judith-edersheim/

Ehlers, A (2015). Understanding and treating unwanted trauma memories in posttraumatic stress disorder. Zeitschrift für Psychologie/*Journal of Psychology*. https://doi.org/10.1027/0044-3409/a000021

Fabian, R., (2019). How art therapy can heal PTSD. Healthline. Available at: https://www.healthline.com/health/art-therapy-for-ptsd

Finkelstein, Y., Sharon, H., Wainstein, G., & Solomon, Z (2022). Avoidance of social cues in posttraumatic stress disorder: An eye-tracking study. Journal of Anxiety Disorders, 86, 102564. https://doi.org/10.1016/j.janxdis.2022.102564

Foa, E. B., Hembree, E. A., & Rothbaum, B. O (2007). Prolonged exposure therapy for PTSD: Emotional processing of traumatic experiences. Guilford Press.

Fleur, K. E., Bloemsma, M. A., & Salemink, E (2022). Avoidance of emotional cues in PTSD: A behavioral and neural investigation. Journal of Abnormal Psychology, 131(3), 273–284. https://doi.org/10.1037/abn0000766

Forrest, W., Edwards, B., & Daraganova, G (2018). The intergenerational consequences of war: Anxiety, depression, suicidality, and mental health among the children of war veterans. *International Journal of Epidemiology, 47*(4), 1060-1067. https://doi.org/10.1093/ije/dyy040

Friedman, M. J (2013). *Finalizing PTSD in DSM-5: Getting here from there and where to go next*. Journal of Traumatic Stress, 26(5), 548-556. https://doi.org/10.1002/jts.21840

Gilles, G (2018). Understanding complex post-traumatic stress disorder. Healthline. https://www.healthline.com/health/cptsd

Gillette, H (2024). Can Post-Traumatic Stress Disorder (PTSD) Cause Irritable Bowel Syndrome? Healthline. https://www.healthline.com/health/ibs/can-ptsd-cause-ibs#prevalence

Goldner, L (2016). Healing through art: PTSD survival stories. PBS SoCal. https://www.pbssocal.org/shows/artbound/healing-through-art-ptsd-survival-stories

Gould, W. R (2023). How to self-soothe when coping with anxiety. Verywell Mind. https://www.verywellmind.com/how-to-self-soothe-when-coping-with-anxiety-5199606

Green, J (2018). Steps to take when your doctor doesn't listen to you - Clara Health. Clara Guides. https://guides.clarahealth.com/steps-when-your-doctor-doesnt-listen/

Grinage, B. D (2003). *Diagnosis and management of post-traumatic stress disorder*. American Family Physician, 68(12), 2401–2409.

Grosso, G., Pajak, A., Marventano, S., Castellano, S., Galvano, F., & Giovannucci, E. L (2014). Role of omega-3 fatty acids in the treatment of depressive disorders: A review. Journal of Affective Disorders, 166, 1-13. doi: 10.1016/j.jad.2014.03.021

Gupta, S., & Mittal, S (2013). Yawning and its physiological significance. Indian Journal of Physiological Pharmacology, 57(1), 93-97. PMID: 23853411

Hanley Center (2023). Complex PTSD and memory loss. Hanley Center. https://www.hanleycenter.org/complex-ptsd-and-memory-loss/

Hensel, J. M., Ruiz, C., Finney, C., & Dewa, C. S (2015). Meta-analysis of risk factors for secondary traumatic stress in therapeutic work with trauma victims. Journal of Traumatic Stress, 28(2), 83-91. https://doi.org/10.1002/jts.21998

Herman, J. L (2015). *Trauma and recovery*. New York, NY: BasicBooks.

Hofmann, S. G., & Hay, A. C (2018). Rethinking avoidance: Toward a balanced approach to avoidance in treating anxiety disorders. *Journal of Anxiety Disorders*, 55(55), 14–21. https://doi.org/10.1016/j.janxdis.2018.03.004

Hofmann, S. G., Asnaani, A., Vonk, I. J., Sawyer, A. T., & Fang, A (2012). The efficacy of cognitive behavioral therapy: A review of meta-analyses. *Cognitive Therapy and Research*, 36(5), 427-440. https://doi.org/10.1007/s10608-012-9476-1

Hofmann, S. G., Sawyer, A. T., Witt, A. A., & Oh, D (2010). The effect of mindfulness-based therapy on anxiety and depression: A meta-analytic review. Journal of Consulting and Clinical Psychology, 78(2), 169-183. doi: 10.1037/a0018555

Holick, M. F (2007). Vitamin D deficiency. New England Journal of Medicine, 357(3), 266-281. doi: 10.1056/NEJMra070553

https://cptsdfoundation.org/2021/03/01/self-harm-and-complex-ptsd/

Jordan, C. G., & Tucker, A (2007). Somatic Experiencing Treatment of Posttraumatic Stress Disorder Symptoms in Hurricane Katrina Survivors: A Pilot Study. Traumatology, 13(2), 13-24. doi: 10.1177/1534765607001300203

Junger, S (2015). How PTSD became a problem far beyond the Battlefield. The Hive; Vanity Fair. https://www.vanityfair.com/news/2015/05/ptsd-war-home-sebastian-junger.

Junger, S., (2022). To Heal PTSD in US Soldiers, First We Have to Heal America, Says Sebastian Junger. Big Think. https://bigthink.com/videos/sebastian-junger-on-ptsd-and-drone-warfare/

Kabat-Zinn, J (2003). Mindfulness-based interventions in context: Past, present, and future. Clinical Psychology: Science and Practice, 10(2), 144-156. doi: 10.1093/clipsy/bpg016

Kaimal, G (n.d.). Girija Kaimal. *American Scientist.* https://www.americanscientist.org/author/girija_kaimal

Kanitz, A (2023). *Generational differences in approaching mental health*. FHE Health. Retrieved from https://fherehab.com/news/generational-differences-mental-health/

Kelly, K., Ratliff, S., & Mezuk, B (2019). Allergies, asthma, and psychopathology in a nationally-representative US sample. Journal of affective disorders, 251, 130-135.

Kendall, S (n.d.). How PTSD affects the aging veteran. *Sean Kendall*. Retrieved from https://www.seankendalllaw.net/blog/ptsd-in-aging-veterans.cfm

Kera-Passante, M (2024). Meditation for PTSD: How it helps & exercises to try. Charlie Health. https://www.charliehealth.com/post/meditation-for-ptsd-how-it-helps-and-exercises-to-try

Kiecolt-Glaser, J. K., & Wilson, S. J (2017). Stress, Skin Aging, and Wound Healing. Journal of Investigative Dermatology, 137(1), e123–e127. doi: 10.1016/j.jid.2016.10.038

King, L. A (2001). The health benefits of writing in positive emotions. Advances in Psychiatric Treatment, 7(5), 346-353. doi: 10.1192/apt.7.5.346

King, L. A (2019). The positive effect of writing on mental health: A randomized controlled trial. Journal of Clinical Psychology, 75(1), 141-152. doi: 10.1002/jclp.22734

Kirschbaum, C., & Hellhammer, D. H (2000). Salivary cortisol in psychological research: an overview. Neuropsychobiology, 42(1-2), 88-103. doi: 10.1159/000026583

Knose, A (2022, December 6). Loving-kindness meditation: Definition, Techniques, & Benefits. Choosing Therapy. https://www.choosingtherapy.com/loving-kindness-meditation/

Kohl, H (2021) Keep up with your daily routines for Improved Mental Health, Acenda. Available at: https://acendahealth.org/blog/keep-up-daily-routines

Kozlowska, K., Walker, P., & Walker, A (2015). Hypnotic reconsolidation of traumatic memories: A new psychotherapeutic approach to treating posttraumatic stress disorder. Journal of Clinical Psychology, 71(1), 1-13. doi: 10.1002/jclp.22133

Levine, P. A (2010). In an Unspoken Voice: How the Body Releases Trauma and Restores Goodness. North Atlantic Books.

Malas, O., & Gómez-Domenech, A (2024). Effect of dialectical behavior therapy on negative affect, and symptoms of depression and anxiety in individuals with borderline personality disorder during the COVID-19 pandemic. *MDPI*. https://shorturl.at/fhmal

Malchiodi, C. A (2015). Art therapy and somatic experience: A qualitative study of art-making and body awareness. Journal of Clinical Art Therapy, 2(1), 1-12.

Margolin, G., & Gordis, E. B (2000). The effects of family and community violence on children. *Annual Review of Psychology, 51*, 445-479. https://doi.org/10.1146/annurev.psych.51.1.445

Marriage, T. A., & Sheffield, B. G (2017). Auditory dysfunction in post-traumatic stress disorder. Journal of Traumatic Stress, 30(2), 133-139. DOI: 10.1002/jts.22173

Mayo Clinic Staff (2022.). Post-traumatic stress disorder (PTSD) - Symptoms and causes. Mayo Clinic. Retrieved from https://www.mayoclinic.org/diseases-conditions/post-traumatic-stress-disorder/symptoms-causes/syc-20355967

McGraw, B (2023). Daily journaling in BSTABLE GO! McGraw Systems. https://www.mcgrawsystems.com/benefits-of-daily-journaling-in-bstable-go/

McLaughlin, K. A., Berglund, P., Gruber, M. J., Kessler, R. C., Sampson, N. A., & Zaslavsky, A. M (2011). Recovery from PTSD following Hurricane Katrina. Depression and Anxiety, 28(6), 439–446. https://doi.org/10.1002/da.20790

Messina, M (2021). Practice cognitive behavioral therapy at home. Dr. Messina & Associates. https://drmessina.com/practice-cognitive-behavioral-therapy-at-home/

Mike Oppland, B (2024). 8 traits of flow according to Mihaly Csikszentmihalyi. PositivePsychology. https://positivepsychology.com/mihaly-csikszentmihalyi-father-of-flow/

Mitchell, J (2020). The Little Blue Rocket Ship: A Story about Postpartum Depression. CreateSpace Independent Publishing Platform.

Mockenhaupt, B (2009). Tragic heroes. The Atlantic. https://www.theatlantic.com/magazine/archive/2009/03/tragic-heroes/307284/

Monson, C. M., & Fredman, S. J (2012). Posttraumatic stress disorder. In A. S. Gurman (Ed.), Clinical handbook of couple therapy (5th ed., pp. 649-673). Guilford Press.

Morina, N., Koerssen, R., & Pollet, T. V (2016). Interventions for children and adolescents with posttraumatic stress disorder: A meta-analysis of comparative outcome studies. *Clinical Psychology Review, 47*, 41-54. https://doi.org/10.1016/j.cpr.2016.05.006

Nagasawa, M., Mitsui, S., En, S., Ohtani, N., Ohta, M., Sakuma, Y., et al (2015). Oxytocin-gaze positive loop and the coevolution of human-dog bonds. *Science*, 348(6232), 333-336. https://doi.org/10.1126/science.1261022

National Academy of Medicine (2019). Vital Directions for Health and Health Care: Priorities From a National Academy of Medicine Initiative. National Academies Press. doi: 10.17226/25467

National Center for PTSD (2019). PTSD and substance abuse in veterans. https://www.ptsd.va.gov/professional/treat/specific/index.asp

National Institute of Mental Health (2024). Post-traumatic stress disorder (PTSD). Retrieved from https://www.nimh.nih.gov/health/topics/post-traumatic-stress-disorder-ptsd

National Institute of Mental Health (n.d.). Post-Traumatic Stress Disorder (PTSD). Retrieved from https://www.nimh.nih.gov/health/topics/post-traumatic-stress-disorder-ptsd/index.shtml

National Institute on Drug Abuse (NIDA) (2020). Principles of Effective Treatment. Retrieved from https://www.drugabuse.gov/publications/principles-drug-addiction-treatment-research-based-guide-third-edition/principles-effective-treatment

Olasove, B (2006). Cognitive-behavioral therapy for adult anxiety disorders: A meta-analysis of randomized placebo-controlled trials. Depression and Anxiety, 23(7), 381-390. doi: 10.1002/da.20155

Pagani, M., Högberg, G., Salmaso, D., & Nardo, D (2013). Neuropsychological and neuroimaging studies of EMDR: A preliminary overview. Journal of EMDR Practice and Research, 7(1), 16-27.

Payne, P., Levine, P. A., & Crane, P (2015). Somatic experiencing: Using interoception and mindfulness to "stay top-down" in the treatment of trauma. Frontiers in Psychology, 6, 1-13.

Pedersen, T (2021). All about Somatic therapy. *Psych Central*. https://psychcentral.com/blog/how-somatic-therapy-can-help-patients-suffering-from-psychological-trauma#how-it-works

Pedersen, T (2022) Emotional dysregulation: Definition, signs, conditions, and coping, *Psych Central*. https://psychcentral.com/blog/what-is-affect-or-emotion-dysregulation

Pedersen, T (2022). Can group therapy help heal trauma? *Psych Central*. Retrieved from https://psychcentral.com/health/can-group-therapy-help-heal-trauma

Philips, P. K (2009). My story of survival: Battling PTSD. Adaa. https://adaa.org/living-with-anxiety/personal-stories/my-story-survival-battling-ptsd

Phillips, S. M., & van Loon, L. J (2011). Dietary protein for athletes: From requirements to optimum adaptation. Journal of

Sports Sciences, 29(S1), S29-S38. doi: 10.1080/02640414.2011.583447

Priest, J. C (2011). Off-duty HPD officer kills daytime intruder at her home. *CHRON*. Retrieved from https://www.chron.com/news/houston-texas/article/Off-duty-HPD-officer-kills-daytime-intruder-at-2079437.php

Psylaris (2021). Negative thoughts due to a traumatic experience. Psylaris. https://psylaris.com/en/trauma-symptoms/negative-thoughts/

Quirke, M. G (2024). *Recovering from complex PTSD: 3 key stages of long-term healing*. Retrieved from https://michaelgquirke.com/recovering-from-complex-ptsd-3-key-stages-of-long-term-healing/

Riva, R., Mork, P. J., Westgaard, R. H., & Lundberg, U (2010). Pain and stress: A systematic review. Scandinavian Journal of Work, Environment & Health, 36(3), 227-239. doi: 10.5271/sjweh.2899

Rosen, G. M., & Lilienfeld, S. O (2016). Posttraumatic stress disorder: An empirical review. Journal of Clinical Psychology, 72(1), 11-33. doi: 10.1002/jclp.22254

Round, E., Wetherell, M. A., Elsey, V., & Smith, M. A (2016). The impact of positive expressive writing on anxiety, well-being, and job satisfaction in a workplace setting. Journal of Workplace Learning, 28(2), 83-95. doi: 10.1108/JWL-05-2015-0035

Rutherford, D (2024). Plant-based trauma recovery:how nutrition diminished my PTSD and chronic pain, BTSADV. https://breakthesilencedv.org/plant-based-trauma-recoveryhow-nutrition-diminished-my-ptsd-and-chronic-pain/

Samuelson, K. W (2011). Post-traumatic stress disorder and declarative memory functioning: a review. Dialogues in clinical neuroscience, 13(3), 346-351.

Sandy (2021). Hyperarousal. NeuRA Library. https://library.neura.edu.au/ptsd-library/signs-and-symptoms-ptsd-library/general-signs-and-symptoms-signs-and-symptoms-ptsd-library/hyperarousal/index.html#:~:text=Hyperarousal%20is%20a%20core%20symptom,difficulty%20concentrating%2C%20and%20difficulty%20sleeping.

Sandy (2010). Negative thoughts and mood. NeuRA Library.: https://library.neura.edu.au/ptsd-library/signs-and-symptoms-ptsd-library/general-signs-and-symptoms-signs-and-symptoms-ptsd-library/negative-alterations-in-cognition-and-mood/index.html

Santrock, J. W (2020). Life-Span Development (17th ed.). McGraw-Hill Education.

Shapiro, F (2017). Eye movement desensitization and reprocessing (EMDR) therapy: Basic principles, protocols, and procedures (3rd ed.). Guilford Press.

Shin, L. M., Rauch, S. L., & Pitman, R. K (2006). Amygdala, medial prefrontal cortex, and hippocampal function in PTSD. Annals of the New York Academy of Sciences, 1071, 67-79. doi: 10.1196/annals.1364.007

Shulman, A (1997). Tinnitus: A Multidisciplinary Approach. Journal of Research in Otolaryngology, 18(1), 1-14.

SingleCare Team (2024). PTSD statistics. SingleCare. Retrieved from https://www.singlecare.com/blog/news/ptsd-statistics/

Spiegel, D (2019). Dissociative identity disorder. Merck Manuals Professional Edition; Merck Manuals. https://www.merckmanuals.com/professional/psychiatric-disorders/dissociative-disorders/dissociative-identity-disorder

Spiegel, D (2023). Dissociative subtype of posttraumatic stress disorder. Merck Manuals Consumer Version. https://www.merckmanuals.com/home/mental-health-disorders/dissociative-disorders/dissociative-subtype-of-posttraumatic-stress-disorder

Stickgold, R (2023). Harvard Catalyst Profiles. Harvard Catalyst. https://connects.catalyst.harvard.edu/Profiles/display/Person/31708

Storm, H (2020). My mental health journey: How PTSD gave me the strength to share my story. Poynter. https://www.poynter.org/business-work/2020/my-mental-health-journey-how-ptsd-gave-me-the-strength-to-share-my-story/

Strauss, J. L., Lang, A. J., & Rousseau, G. S (2014). Mindfulness-based treatments for posttraumatic stress disorder: A systematic review. Journal of Clinical Psychology, 70(1), 1-14. doi: 10.1002/jclp.22036

Taché, Y., & Yang, H (2018). Role of corticotropin-releasing factor in the gut-brain axis. Journal of Clinical Gastroenterology, 52(8), 537-543. doi: 10.1097/MCG.0000000000000966

U.S. Department of Veterans Affairs (2023). Common problems for veterans with PTSD. Retrieved from https://www.ptsd.va.gov/understand/common/common_adults.asp

U.S. Veterans Magazine (2023). Seo Title Preview: I'm a Vietnam War veteran. here's how writingmy memoir has helped me heal. U.S. Veterans Magazine. https://usveteransmagazine.com/usvm/im-vietnam-war-veteran-heres-writing-memoir-helped-heal/

Ullman, S. E (1996). Social reactions, coping strategies, and self-blame attributions in adjustment to sexual assault. Psychology of Women Quarterly, 20(2), 505-526. doi: 10.1111/j.1471-6402.1996.tb00319.x

Uttekar, P.S (n.d.). How does emotion affect cognition? MedicineNet. https://www.medicinenet.com/how_does_emotion_affect_cognition/article.htm

Van der Kolk, B. A (2014). The Body Keeps the Score: Brain, Mind, and Body in the Healing of Trauma. Viking.

Van Der Pluym, S (2019). Strategies to reduce dissociation. *New View Psychology.* https://newviewpsychology.com.au/strategies-to-reduce-dissociation/

Vickers, M. H (2015). PTSD and the workplace: A review of the literature. Journal of Workplace Behavioral Health, 30(2), 133-144. https://doi.org/10.1080/15555240.2015.1025124

Wick, J. Y (2021). Impact of trauma on aging baby boomers. *HCP Live.* https://www.hcplive.com/view/impact-of-trauma-on-aging-baby-boomers

Yehuda, R., Daskalakis, N. P., Bierer, L. M., Bader, H. N., Klengel, T., Holsboer, F., & Meaney, M. J (2016). Holocaust exposure induced intergenerational effects on FKBP5 methylation. Biological Psychiatry, 80(5), 372-380.

Zorzi, V. D (2023). Author and war reporter Sebastian Junger '80 speaks about crisis and courage at CA. Concord Academy. Retrieved from https://concordacademy.org/author-and-war-reporter-sebastian-junger-80-speaks/

Gerten, K. (2021, June 2). It's Survival. 13 Quotes On Trauma & Healing. Retrieved from https://www.youthdynamics.org/its-survival-13-quotes-on-trauma-healing/

Judy Siegel Itzkovich (2024, December 1). Israel's world-leading hyperbaric chamber performing medical 'miracles'. https://www.jpost.com/health-and-wellness/article-831392

www.ingramcontent.com/pod-product-compliance
Lightning Source LLC
LaVergne TN
LVHW061617070526
838199LV00078B/7311